PALACE · CARS ✛

COACHES

MINNEAPOLIS AND ST. PAUL

MAP OF THE
Iowa Central
RAILWAY COMPANY
AND CONNECTIONS

Palace Sleeping Cars

BETWEEN
ST. PAUL,
MINNEAPOLIS
AND
PEORIA,
MOBERLY,
KANSAS CITY
AND
ST. LOUIS,
WITH DIRECT CONNECTIONS IN
UNION DEPOT TO AND FROM
PRINCIPAL POINTS
IN
MINNESOTA,
NORTH DAKOTA,
SOUTH DAKOTA,
MONTANA,
MANITOBA,
WASHINGTON,
OREGON
AND
MISSOURI,
KANSAS,
COLORADO,
ILLINOIS,
ARKANSAS,
INDIANA,
OHIO,
KENTUCKY,
TENNESSEE,
MISSISSIPPI,
TEXAS,
LOUISIANA
AND
FLORIDA.

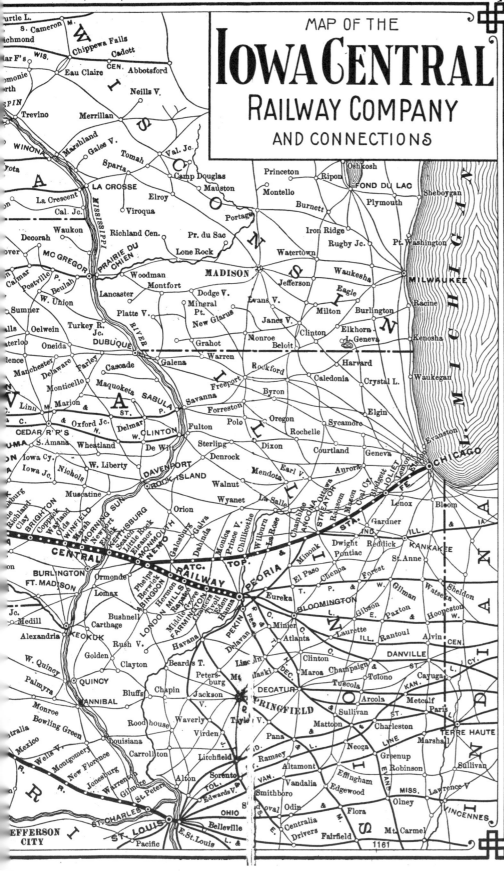

1161

THE HOOK & EYE

THE HOOK & EYE

A History of the Iowa Central Railway

Don L. Hofsommer

University of Minnesota Press
Minneapolis • London

Published by the University of Minnesota Press
111 Third Avenue South, Suite 290
Minneapolis, MN 55401-2520
http://www.upress.umn.edu

Library of Congress Cataloging-in-Publication Data

Hofsommer, Donovan L.
    The Hook & Eye : a history of the Iowa Central Railway / Don L. Hofsommer.
        p.   cm.
    Includes bibliographical references and index.
    ISBN 0-8166-4497-7 (hc/j : alk. paper)
    1. Iowa Central Railway—History.   I. Title: Hook and Eye.   II. Title.
    HE2791.I683H64 2005
    385'.09777'09034—dc22

                                                                2005004875

Printed in the United States of America on acid-free paper

The University of Minnesota is an equal-opportunity educator and employer.

12 11 10 09 08 07 06 05   10 9 8 7 6 5 4 3 2 1

For
Howard V. Jones
Erma B. Plaehn
Leland L. Sage
who had faith and showed the way

Contents

PREFACE

IN THE EARLY TWENTY-FIRST CENTURY, RAILWAYS have mostly faded from national consciousness. They handle more freight tonnage than ever before, but garner only a small fraction of the transportation dollar, and Amtrak carries fewer than 1 percent of intercity passengers. This is a precipitous change from an era not far removed from this, when railways were at the center of the American stage, creating a steamcar civilization. Indeed they were the country's first big business; many roads were the bluest of blue-chip investments. Iowa Central was part of this mosaic—more than a bit player, to be sure, but never a crucial element in the national fabric. Its earliest predecessor, Eldora Railroad & Coal Company, represented parochial purposes of moving locally mined coal to nearby markets. This limited raison d'être quickly ballooned to an expansive dream of becoming an integral link in an important Minnesota–to–St. Louis route that would challenge the dominance of Chicago and its aggressive railroads, which had laced Iowa with powerful horizontal arteries. Those aspirations were not met, although Minneapolis & St. Louis, Iowa Central's successor, did forge an efficient and useful Minneapolis–Peoria option that circumvented

Chicago. In the end, Iowa Central's 560 route miles served primarily local needs, mirroring the life and purpose of most American rail lines. But this was hardly inconsequential: after all, Iowa Central and its predecessors gave birth to several communities and gave advantage to others while opening monumental marketing opportunities for agriculturalists and industrialists. Iowa Central and its predecessors and successors provided essential transportation to a broad constituency during the years of modal monopoly, and afterward were important consumers of all manner of supplies and equipment, were major taxpayers in Iowa and Illinois as well as in all counties and municipalities in the service area, and gave employment to thousands of people over the years.

This study singles out Iowa Central as a vehicle to investigate the inception, growth, evolution, and eventual disappearance (by merger) of a regional carrier in the upper Midwest during the age of railways. The operation of Iowa Central was always plain vanilla—but vital—and was typical of the operation of unremarked rail lines around the country at the time. An important theme here is the struggle of Iowa Central and its corporate ancestors to carve out a transportation niche as a vertical-axis carrier in a geographic area dominated by a grid of horizontal roads and to offer Minneapolis and St. Louis as competitive alternatives to Chicago. The experience of Iowa Central lines during the period when it was owned by Minneapolis & St. Louis and afterward is related in my book *The Tootin' Louie: A History of the Minneapolis & St. Louis Railway,* also published by the University of Minnesota Press.

A nearly endless stream of generous people have helped me in this endeavor, a fact that gives me great pleasure and gratification. I retain warm memories of interviews with persons in places from Ackley to Zearing and from Northwood to Peoria—active and retired railroaders, farmers, waitresses, shippers, and others who willingly shared recollections of people and events germane to this study. LaVerne W. Andreessen, Vaughn R. Ward, and H. Roger Grant are among many others who gave support and counsel. Paul H. Stringham answered numerous requests for assistance, as did Frank P. Donovan Jr. Most of all I am indebted to Professor Leland L. Sage, whose constant aid and encouragement remain for me a model of mentoring. To all mentioned here, and to others whom I regrettably have overlooked, I am deeply grateful. For errors of fact and infelicities of style that remain, I alone am responsible.

ACRONYMS AND SHORTENED NAMES

A&C	Albia & Centerville	**CR&MR**	Cedar Rapids & Missouri River
AT&SF	Atchison, Topeka & Santa Fe	**CRCI**	Central Railroad Company of Iowa
B&MR	Burlington & Missouri River	**CRI&P**	Chicago, Rock Island & Pacific
B&W	Burlington & Western		
BCR&M	Burlington, Cedar Rapids & Minnesota	**D&SC**	Dubuque & Sioux City
		DMV	Des Moines Valley
BCR&N	Burlington, Cedar Rapids & Northern	**ER&CC**	Eldora Railroad & Coal Company
Burlington Route	Chicago, Burlington & Quincy	**G&M**	Grinnell & Montezuma
C&NW	Chicago & North Western	**Hook & Eye**	Central Railroad Company of Iowa
CB&P	Chicago, Burlington & Pacific		Central Iowa Railway
			Iowa Central Railway
CB&Q	Chicago, Burlington & Quincy	**IC**	Illinois Central
		IC&NW	Iowa Central & Northwestern
The Central	Central Railroad Company of Iowa		
	Central Iowa Railway	**M&NW**	Minnesota & Northwestern
	Iowa Central Railway		
CF&M	Cedar Falls & Minnesota	**M&StL**	Minneapolis & St. Louis
CI	Central Iowa	**MI&N**	Missouri, Iowa & Nebraska
CM&A	Centerville, Moravia & Albia	**Milwaukee Road**	Chicago, Milwaukee & St. Paul
CM&StP	Chicago, Milwaukee & St. Paul	**North Western**	Chicago & North Western

P&F	Peoria & Farmington	**Santa Fe**	Atchison, Topeka & Santa Fe
Plug	Eldora Railroad & Coal Company	**SP**	Southern Pacific
		StL&CR	St. Louis & Cedar Rapids
Rock Island	Chicago, Rock Island & Pacific		

Chapter 1
URBAN MERCANTILISM

With the use of a map, any person can see that all the [rail]roads and branches
that we have noticed aim at Chicago from east and west, north and south.
It is the great center which they all seek. Let them come!
—Chicago Daily Democratic Press, annual review pamphlet for 1852

AT THE BEGINNING OF THE NINETEENTH century, President Thomas Jefferson saw in the mostly untapped wilderness west of the Mississippi River a huge expanse that might for a time serve as a giant Indian preserve and eventually as a rich domain into which vibrant Americans could pour as the rate of settling land in the East demanded it. With that in mind, in 1803 he secured from France the vast territory of the Louisiana Purchase, which extended from the Mississippi to the Rockies. But not even the prescient Jefferson foresaw the rapidity with which that western country would be populated. In 1821 Missouri became the first state carved fully out of the Louisiana Purchase; Arkansas followed in 1836, Iowa in 1846, Minnesota in 1858. Several variables combined in this astonishingly swift development, but none proved more prominent than the veritable revolution in transportation that swept the country following the War of 1812.[1]

In 1823 the steamboat *Virginia,* upbound from St. Louis to Fort Snelling, spewed its hot breath abroad the upper Mississippi to introduce that revolutionary technology along what became Iowa's eastern border. The *Virginia*'s voyage represented the economic

imperial instincts of St. Louis and the earliest manifestation of desires to link that place with what became the twin Minnesota cities of St. Paul and Minneapolis. There was no doubting the impact of steamboating on the transportation traditions of the new republic and on acceleration of the westering process, but in northern climes winter shut down waterborne commerce for weeks and even months. Moreover, in all instances these vessels were restricted to navigable water, which was limited in most areas and totally absent in others. All of these factors were reflected in Iowa, where steamboats did a bountiful business at Keokuk, Dubuque, and other locations along the Mississippi and could be found on the Des Moines River and elsewhere. Yet the bulk of the state, like most of the trans-Mississippi West, urgently awaited the age of railways, which would not be long in coming.[2]

During the winter of 1836–37, one John Plumbe called a meeting at Dubuque to "discuss the railroad question." Those in attendance heard Plumbe passionately advocate "the feasibility of the construction of a railroad from Milwaukee to Dubuque, as a link by which the lakes would be connected with the Mississippi." At least one man who heard his oration proclaimed Plumbe a visionary; others, though, felt his views "might have been a little premature." Undaunted, Plumbe continued his efforts, and on March 26, 1838, he was joined by other prominent Dubuque citizens in drafting a memorial to Congress seeking appointment of an engineer to locate a rail route to Dubuque from Milwaukee. This memorial was duly presented to the U.S. House of Representatives on May 21, 1838, by Territorial Delegate George Wallace Jones, and was greeted with a "great laugh and hurrah in the house, members singing out . . . that it would not be long before . . . constituents would ask Congress to build a railroad to the moon." Nevertheless, lawmakers did appropriate a small sum of money, and a survey was undertaken.[3]

To the farsighted John Plumbe, the Milwaukee–Dubuque effort was merely a significant fraction of his total vision. In 1836 he had traveled west, and the idea of a railroad to the Pacific Ocean had germinated in his fertile mind. He was to spend the remainder of his life championing that cause. While Plumbe's efforts were earlier and more dramatic than most, his thinking served to exemplify the fact that "railroad fever," which had enveloped the East during the early 1830s, moved swiftly westward into the area that in 1846 became the state of Iowa. Indeed, virtually all hands recognized the tyranny of distance in the infant republic. Roads of rail, they quickly came to understand, would provide transportation salvation; steamcars would provide reliable, low-cost, all-season, high-speed means of transporting passengers, express, mail, and light freight. They further recognized that rails alone were adequate to provide overland transport of heavy lading—lumber, fuel, and grain, for example—in a way that would not consume the value of those commodities in carriage charges; that transportation channels were the necessary cardio-vascular system for the national body; and that rails

could serve as powerful sinews binding disparate regions together as one.[4]

Iowa's marvelous Ice Age gifts—bountiful and rich soil that inevitably lured the plowman—alone would have attracted rails. In 1836 Lieutenant Albert M. Lea described Iowa country as a grand rolling prairie interspersed with rivers, lakes, and woods. All in all, said Lea, "for convenience of navigation, water, fuel, and timber, for richness of soil; for beauty of appearance; and for pleasantness of climate, it surpasses any portion of the United States with which I am acquainted." Lea's appraisal was echoed in chorus by others. Iowa's population jumped from 22,859 in 1838 to 43,112 in 1840, and to 96,088 in the statehood year of 1846; settlement was found in roughly half of what became ninety-nine counties. The capital was sited at Iowa City.[5]

There were, however, variables in addition to Iowa's agricultural potential that exerted powerful influences on the ultimate development of the state's railroad network. These eventually included the rise of Minneapolis/St. Paul and Kansas City as substantial industrial, commercial, and transportation centers, but more immediately entailed the aggressive impulses and growing competition between St. Louis and Chicago—especially as those two aspirants scrambled for advantage relative to any transcontinental railroad. That crucial issue, however, got completely embroiled in sectional tension surrounding the possible expansion of slavery into the western territories. No decision on the eastern terminus of the transcontinental rail line or on its route west would be forthcoming in the 1850s.[6]

The nation's rails nevertheless pushed ever westward. Chicago, a tiny community of 4,470 persons in 1840, grew to a population of 29,963 in 1850, and already had one railroad, a predecessor of Chicago & North Western (C&NW or North Western), inching westward from that city toward Galena and the lead-mining region of northwestern Illinois—and this was before rails reached Chicago from the east. That was only the beginning. Illinois Central (IC), a vertical axis road that would be driven from north to south down the center of that state, also would feature one branch to Chicago and another to Dunleith, which lay across the Mississippi from Dubuque. Another road, Chicago, Burlington & Quincy (CB&Q or Burlington Route), promised to link Chicago with the Mississippi River communities of Quincy and Burlington. And Chicago & Rock Island—later Chicago, Rock Island & Pacific (CRI&P or Rock Island)—pledged to put down track that, when completed, would end up opposite Davenport.[7]

Chicago leaders fully embraced steamcars as the appropriate means to capture wealth from a huge hinterland; Chicago-based roads with lines pressing westward to the Mississippi River reflected as much. Denizens of St. Louis were hardly unmindful of that city's own opportunities for economic imperialism through railroad expansion, but they remained deeply devoted to river navigation. Strategically located on the Mississippi just south of confluences with the Illinois and the Missouri and above its confluence with the Ohio, St. Louis earned early dominion over a giant backcountry. Prominent observers forecast great things for St. Louis, and its claim as the "Gateway City" was hard to dispute with the constant fever of activity on its levees, where riverboat cargoes were unloaded, loaded, or transloaded. Just as New York City had used the Hudson and Mohawk Rivers along with the Erie Canal for its economic conquests, so did St. Louis use the Mississippi and its tributaries in the same fashion. By 1840, St. Louis provided about half the marketing and supply needs of Illinois, and St. Louis leaders took pride in the trade inroads made in what would become the states of Iowa, Wisconsin, and Minnesota.[8]

It would be Chicago, however, that would come to the fullest dominance of the midcontinent. In 1860, St. Louis would register a population of over 160,000, greater than Chicago's 110,000, but the tide of commerce would already be tilting dramatically toward Chicago and away from St. Louis. The years of awful civil war only accelerated that process. Again the Chicago-based railroads standing on the eastern shores of the Mississippi reflected as much. Iowa's railroad mileage during the 1850s leapt from 0 to 655, most of it put down across the rolling prairie of the state's eastern reaches by surrogates or friends of Chicago roads. By 1861, CB&Q's Iowa puppet (Burlington & Missouri River) had extended itself from Burlington to Ottumwa; Rock Island's client (Mississippi & Missouri) stood at Iowa City after completing a line from Davenport; C&NW's ally (Chicago, Iowa & Nebraska) had reached out from Clinton to Cedar Rapids; and IC's feeder (Dubuque & Sioux City) had steamed out from Dubuque to Waterloo. In addition, a pioneer line of what would become Chicago, Milwaukee & St. Paul (CM&StP or Milwaukee Road) stretched across southern Wisconsin from Milwaukee to Prairie du Chien with clear designs on the rich lands west of the Mississippi. Elsewhere, a promising independent, Des Moines Valley (DMV) struggled northwestward from Keokuk, reaching Eddyville in 1861. All of these except DMV and the hopeful Milwaukee interloper represented Chicago interests whose roads, in time, bridged the Mississippi to link Illinois and Iowa operations, forwarding trainloads of lumber and all manner of manufactured goods westward while receiving in return trainloads of grain and livestock.[9]

The power of Chicago and its railroads and their influence on Iowa and its citizens only increased when the central overland route was selected for the first transcontinental rail line and Council Bluffs was designated as its eastern terminus. The Civil War curtailed most Iowa railroad construction, but when peace came in 1865, officers of Chicago clients became frantic in the race to reach Council Bluffs and partner with Union Pacific on long-haul business. The winner was Cedar Rapids & Missouri River, C&NW's surrogate, which reached Council Bluffs on January 22, 1867; the second to arrive was Rock Island, on May 11, 1869, one day after the final spike was driven at Promontory Summit to open the country's first transcontinental route. A Burlington predecessor arrived to begin service on January 1, 1870. So three Chicago roads met Union Pacific at Council Bluffs and solidified horizontal arteries of commerce across the state from east to west.[10]

All of this was adequate to set off euphoric celebration both near at hand and far away. Indeed, during the early age of railways nothing was more to be desired than the steamcars. But in Iowa, many residents became nervous in an environment dominated by Chicago roads and those who controlled them. Competition, they argued, was the appropriate antidote—not just the competition that might be offered by those same Chicago roads by means of branches and feeders that they could throw out, but rather the competition of roads emanating from and reflecting interests of other metropolitan contenders—of which St. Louis was the most prominent alternative. Minnesotans had similar feelings, fearing the power of Chicago and yearning for a rail chute linking St. Paul and Minneapolis with St. Louis. And St. Louis moguls in the postwar era became fully alert to advantages of such a link. Potential synergies were obvious: Iowa would provide grain for the hungry flouring mills at St. Anthony Falls and coal for fuel-starved Minnesota; Minnesota would provide milled lumber and high-grade flour for Iowa and Missouri markets; and St. Louis would supply mercantile goods and manufactured items of all sorts for Iowa and Minnesota consumers. All of this would be at the expense of Chicago and its lusting iron tentacles. So went the argument, and nowhere was it more enthusiastically promoted than in central Iowa.

Chapter 2

IOWA CENTRAL RAILROAD: GREAT PLANS, GRAND FAILURE

Everything looks favorable and is working well for the
Iowa Central Railroad—the Grand Trunk Railway of the West.
—CEDAR FALLS GAZETTE, JUNE 1, 1866

THE STATE OF IOWA WAS THE SCENE OF IN-tense railroad activity during the mid-nineteenth century. Many efforts were fostered by dreamers and schemers of Chicago persuasion, each bent on a fervid campaign to promote that city's interests by way of an expansive railway network. Promoting and building of these east-west, or horizontal, roads then was augmented by another flurry of railroad planning and construction that had as its purpose the connection of prominent Midwestern cities lying to the north and to the south of Iowa. Indeed, efforts to build a series of east-west roads across the state, and to overlay them in grid fashion with north-south, or vertical, lines, represented the opening chapter in Iowa's railroad era. One such vertical route, the Iowa Central Railroad—an enterprise designed to link the Hawkeye State with St. Louis on the south and with St. Paul on the north—was enthusiastically hailed by its promoters as "the grandest railroad project of the age." It promised much, but in the end was "grand" only in its failure as one of the most important of the proposed vertical railroads across Iowa.[1]

The precursor of the Iowa Central Railroad

was the aptly named St. Louis, Iowa & St. Paul Railway. The goals of this company were clearly implied in its name—to join St. Louis with St. Paul over a route serving the Iowa communities of Oskaloosa, Toledo, and Cedar Falls. Interest along the projected road was understandably keen. As one writer put it, "Such a road would supply central Iowa with its two greatest needs, coal from southern Iowa and cheap building material from Minnesota." Nevertheless, the panic of 1857, the Civil War, and the subsequent secession depression all combined to forestall construction; the company lost its franchise before a single rail had been laid.[2]

Interest in a north-south road through central Iowa did not flag, however. Even before the Civil War ended, a new company—the Iowa Central Railroad—was formed on January 5, 1865. This enterprise was capitalized at $6 million; its headquarters were to be in Oskaloosa. The company's charter called for construction and operation of a road reaching from the terminus of the North Missouri Railroad on the southern border of Iowa to a connection with the Cedar Falls & Minnesota Railroad (CF&M) at Cedar Falls. The company's first president was one of its earliest and most energetic boosters—David Morgan, a resident of New Sharon, Iowa.

Morgan was particularly optimistic during the summer of 1865. He had good reason. Risk capital was increasingly available, there was expanding public confidence in railroads, and there was general local support for the project. The sale of Iowa Central stock commenced during the same season; volume was strong. Moreover, there was good news from both Minnesota and Missouri. Rails of the Minnesota Central Railway, a predecessor of Chicago, Milwaukee & St. Paul, already extended some seventy miles to the south of St. Paul, and construction on the remaining portion would soon close the gap to the Iowa border. To the south, the North Missouri Railroad was already operating trains over 170 miles of completed trackage between St. Louis and Macon, Missouri. Only a

brief construction drive would be necessary to bring its service to the Iowa frontier. To be sure, the large gap on the St. Louis–St. Paul route was in Iowa, where only the fifteen miles between Cedar Falls and Waverly, operated by Cedar Falls & Minnesota, were in service.[3]

During the summer of 1865, the editor of the *Cedar Falls Gazette* wondered who, if anybody, could be "stupid enough to fear that the Iowa Central will not be built, when the people of Iowa from Cedar Falls to the State Line [of Missouri] are bleeding so outrageously from the monopolies of heartless railroad corporations?" These corporations were, of course, the Chicago-based horizontal carriers.[4]

Chicago, or at least the perceived nefarious activities of its merchants and railroad men, was at the heart of much north-south railroad sentiment in Iowa. The editor of the *Cedar Falls Gazette*, for

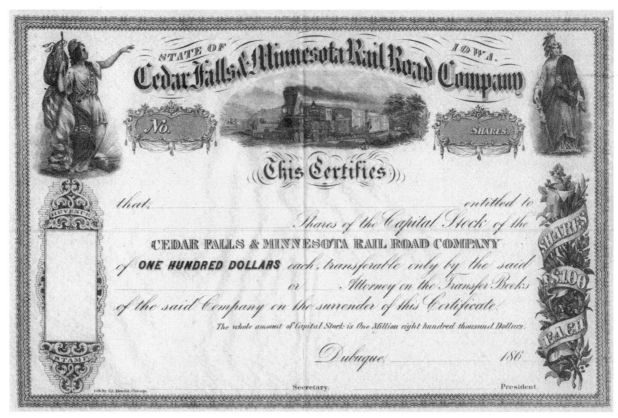

Figure 2.1. The *Cedar Falls Gazette* pinned its hopes on Cedar Falls & Minnesota to provide adequate competition in conjunction with others forming a Minneapolis–St. Louis route.

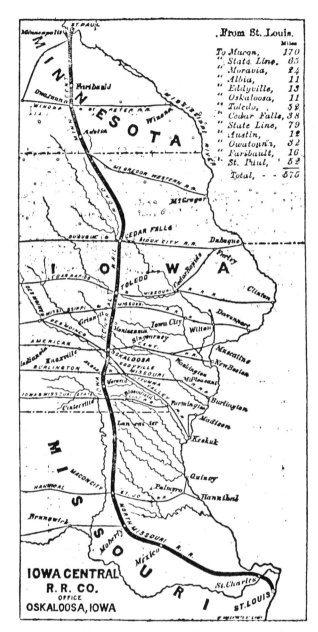

From St. Louis.

		Miles
To	Macon,	170
"	State Line,	85
"	Moravia,	24
"	Albia,	11
"	Eddyville,	13
"	Oskaloosa,	11
"	Toledo,	52
"	Cedar Falls,	38
"	State Line,	79
"	Austin,	12
"	Owatonna,	32
"	Faribault,	16
"	St. Paul,	52
	Total,	575

IOWA CENTRAL
R. R. CO.
OFFICE
OSKALOOSA, IOWA

Map 2.1. Would Iowa Central Railroad become, as one of its officers asserted, "The Grand Trunk Railway of the West"?

and in his judgment they left nothing "undone to prevent shipments to and from St. Louis." The only answer to the problem, in his view and in the eyes of many Iowans, was a road to St. Louis; this would reduce Iowans' dependence on Chicago by placing the market of St. Louis in direct competition.[5]

A St. Louis outlet would "at once place in competition for our trade the two greatest grain markets in the world, and place us in a commanding position, instead of the subservient one we now occupy," exclaimed the *Gazette*'s editor. Moreover, railroad communication with St. Louis would ensure that the merchants of mid-Iowa would be able to sell most of their goods as inexpensively as those purveyed currently by Chicago concerns. Farmers, too, would benefit. Quick calculation showed that with an all-rail route to St. Louis farmers would gain from 15 to 25 cents more per bushel of grain than they were then receiving in Chicago.[6]

Iowa Central promoters consistently hammered on a recurring theme: rival railroads—if Chicago-based or tied only to that outlet—were inadequate; what was required were rival railroads serving rival cities. The editor of the *Gazette* put it simply: "Competition is the only panacea for all monopolies."[7]

Many additional arguments were offered in favor of Iowa Central. One Black Hawk County farmer contended, for instance, that the value of real estate along the proposed line would appreciate by no less than one-third as soon as construction began. He asserted that farmland within a convenient distance of the road would rise from $5 to $10 per acre. Furthermore, according to the *Gazette,* the road would give farmers both a winter market and year-round water transportation from St. Louis to all parts of the globe; Iowa consumers would be able to receive goods from the South as inexpensively as could Chicago consumers; during the navigation season, products of the industrialized Ohio River valley could be delivered inexpensively to Iowa consumers via St. Louis; lumber and the

example, was utterly convinced that area citizens had been unnecessarily victimized by business interests of Chicago. Indeed, he bellowed, Chicago railroads and produce buyers had been engaged in the "pernicious practice of deceiving the people of Iowa, in various respects, in the purchase of the surplus products of the state." He further growled, in a mix of irritation and exasperation, that "Chicago interests" controlled virtually all of the Iowa roads, products of Lake Superior mines could be efficiently transported to Iowa customers; and with the new road in operation, there would be no need for the time-consuming and inefficient practices of breaking bulk and ferrying cars at Dubuque. The *Gazette* summed up by asserting that Iowa Central was a local enterprise dedicated to the idea of doing for Iowa what Illinois Central had done for Illinois; that traffic in Mahaska and Monroe County coal plus shipments of pine from the north alone would be adequate to sustain the road; and that its construction would allow Iowans to buy everything at a lower price and sell everything for a higher price than was then the case.[8]

Interest in the road was both keen and widespread. Governor William H. Stone was an enthusiastic backer of the project, and on March 3, 1866, with only one vote in dissent, the Iowa legislature addressed a memorial to Congress asking for a grant of land to aid in construction of the road. The legislators emphasized that a north-south road would engender competition and thus reduce rates: "It would be the best regulator of excessive tariffs." They saw in Iowa Central an important link in a "great chain of railroads from the lakes of the north to the Gulf on the south," a chain with its northern terminus at Superior City and its southern terminus at Galveston, tapping both St. Louis and St. Paul, and, incidentally, serving Iowa as it bridged the state on a vertical axis. On March 28, 1866, the memorial was referred to the Committee on Public Lands in the House of Representatives. Representative Josiah B. Grinnell told William T. Smith, who had succeeded David Morgan as president of Iowa Central, that he thought Congress would act affirmatively.[9]

Meanwhile, the president of Minnesota Central assured officials of Iowa Central that a connection of the two roads was "regarded as of the first importance" by his company. Minnesota Governor William R. Marshall similarly assured Iowa Central officials of his state's interest in the road. Minneso-

ta's aspirations, he affirmed, were similar to Iowa's: securing a direct all-weather route to St. Louis, securing access to southern as well as world markets, and securing a competing line to the East. All of this was gratifying, of course, but firm support from the South was equally important to the success of the Iowa Central venture.[10]

Leading citizens of St. Louis had not been unmindful of Iowa Central and its potential benefit to them. They knew that during the Civil War considerable trade from the North had been lost by St. Louis to Chicago, and they knew that Chicago-based railroads had facilitated much of this loss. St. Louis interests now hoped to recapture that trade, and some of its leading men anticipated that Iowa Central could be the prime mover in that effort.[11]

At a gathering of Iowa Central boosters in Oskaloosa on April 27, 1865, a decision was made to send a delegation to St. Louis, and it was warmly received on June 21 at a meeting of over 150 railroad men and St. Louis capitalists at the Lindell Hotel. One of the results of the meeting was that the city of St. Louis and the state of Missouri collectively promised to do their parts in binding Iowa and Missouri together by rail. Isaac H. Sturgeon, president of the North Missouri Railroad, reminded those present that peace had come, that slavery was dead, and that St. Louis was alive to her opportunities. He also pledged his personal interest and the corporate efforts of his railroad to assist Iowa Central.[12]

Such news was adequate to set off a wave of euphoria all along the proposed route. Enthusiasm reached its zenith when Iowa Central officials announced a groundbreaking ceremony for September 19 at Cedar Falls. It proved a gala celebration. Streets were crowded with spectators anxious to applaud the 1,500 parade participants and, to be sure, the reason for the parade itself. A bandwagon was particularly well received; on its sides, in red capital letters, flamed the words "Iowa Central." And in the procession or along its route were a number of persons waving banners proclaiming a great variety of homilies and slogans, including these:

> The Lakes And Gulf Have Met, Shook Hands, and Vowed Eternal Friendship
>
> The New Trinity—Minnesota, Iowa, and Missouri
>
> The Direct Route to All Parts of the Old World Is the Iowa Central via St. Louis
>
> The Strongest Ties between North and South Are the Iowa Central Ties
>
> The Roads That Pay—New York Central, Michigan Central, Illinois Central, and Iowa Central

The procession moved south—symbolically toward Missouri—where, at the edge of town, dirt was turned to initiate construction of the Iowa Central Railroad. Thereafter followed the customary speeches and feasting; a grand ball completed the celebration.[13]

Exuberance went unabated. At Cedar Falls, storefronts advertised the Iowa Central Hall of Fashions, the Iowa Central Iron Works, and the Iowa Central Agricultural Warehouse & Seed Store. Meanwhile, local musicians organized the Iowa Central Band. Moreover, there was also tangible evidence of the project. Indeed, a contract was let for grading and bridging of the first ten miles south from Cedar Falls. It was followed by another on November 1, in Tama County, for the road north of Toledo toward Cedar Falls. Of particular note was news that Tama County voters had approved a $40,000 bond issue in favor of Iowa Central, and that it had agreed to grant the road some 30,000 acres of county swamplands. At about the same time, Appanoose County voters in southern Iowa

Figure 2.2. The ceremonial breaking of ground for the Iowa Central Railroad as depicted by *Frank Leslie's Illustrated Newspaper,* October 21, 1865.

approved bonds in the amount of $50,000, plus considerable swampland scrip.[14]

As the year 1865 came to a close, progress reports remained favorable. Supporters of the road were especially encouraged when they learned that the North Missouri Railroad was surveying northward from Macon to the Iowa border. And President Sturgeon of the Missouri company reminded an official of Iowa Central that his road had full faith in the Iowa firm. There was no mention of any financial support for Iowa Central, however. That seemed to matter little in that happy Christmas season of 1865.[15]

During the next year, Iowa Central officials continued to seek support for the St. Louis–St. Paul railroad—"one of the great wants of the state," according to Peter Melendy, the firm's vice president. Melendy's assertion was well-founded: eighty-three of Iowa's most prominent men had recently signed an impressive memorial to capitalists of St. Louis entitled "Iowa Central Railroad—Why It Should Be Built." It had a most desirable effect. North Missouri's board of directors responded by adopting the following resolution:

> The North Missouri Railroad hereby pledges itself to extend every facility tending to encourage the success of such enterprise. . . . It will aid, assist and give its influence in behalf of the Iowa Central Railroad. . . . We regard it as one of the most important railway enterprises to St. Louis. . . . This company will, so far as it may have any ability to do so, aid in the purchase of iron for the track of said railroad, and the equipping of it with rolling stock, and . . . it will not in its business or time-tables, discriminate against the Iowa Central in favor of any other railroad.

Perhaps with this in mind, Iowa Central's A. D. Barnum wrote to an on-line editor, advising him, "Everything looks favorable and is working well for the Iowa Central Railroad—*The Grand Trunk Railway of the West!*"[16]

The St. Louis resolution was heartily endorsed along the route of the Iowa road. At Albia persons attending a promotional meeting agreed that the time had come for energetic action in support of the road. Farther north, eighty-nine men and thirty teams labored on the first ten miles of grade out of Cedar Falls. And in June 1866, a second groundbreaking ceremony was held on the Iowa-Missouri border. Iowa Central President W. T. Smith stood with one foot in Missouri and the other in Iowa, and with a single scoop of his shovel turned soil of the two states. All looked well. In July, a rumor that the great Philadelphia firm of Jay Cooke & Company was interested in the project floated along the line. By December, the village of Eddyville had fulfilled its subscriptions, and a contract was let for the right-of-way between that community and the Missouri border. The entire route of the Iowa Central had been surveyed, except for a portion in Poweshiek County around Grinnell, where various parties yet contested for the road. By the end of 1866, 90 percent of the 151 miles between Cedar Falls and the Missouri frontier was under contract, and thirty-eight miles were ready for ties.[17]

But all was not well. The Cedar Falls & Minnesota Railroad, with which Iowa Central expected to connect at Cedar Falls as a part of the St. Louis–St. Paul route, had come under the influence of the Dubuque & Sioux City Railroad (D&SC), an east-west road, and in fact CF&M was leased to D&SC on September 22, 1866. For that matter, D&SC itself would be leased to the Chicago-based Illinois Central Railroad on October 1, 1867. All of this properly frightened Iowa Central promoters, because they feared "foreigners" might throttle the local road and in the process subvert the purposes of the St. Louis–St. Paul route. To avoid any potential difficulties in interchanging traffic with an unfriendly or indifferent carrier for the Cedar

Falls–Minnesota border segment, the Iowa Central Railroad Construction Company was formed on April 16, 1866. Capitalized at $6 million, it was authorized to construct, maintain, and operate a railroad from Cedar Falls to a connection with the Minnesota Central Railroad at or near the Iowa-Minnesota border. The Iowa Central Railroad Construction Company was independent of the Iowa Central Railroad, but many of its directors were also associated with the latter firm, and it clearly was a puppet. The entire distance from Iowa's northern border to its southern border now would be in the hands of a single carrier, but the need to protect the northern connection added seventy-seven more route-miles and, simultaneously, the necessity of seeking even more funding.[18]

Regrettably for Iowa Central, the problems on the north were not the only ones it faced. As early as the summer of 1865, the editor of the *Cedar Falls Gazette* had observed that it "was unreasonable to suppose that a great central road will be built across Iowa without much clashing of localities, and much wire-pulling and hard work for the furtherance of public and private interests of various sections." He might have added that not every Iowa community favored the Iowa Central project. Mississippi River cities did not, for they stood to lose much in water traffic if the railroad was built. Nor did the archrival of Cedar Falls, nearby Waterloo, favor the road, for Iowa Central would not pass through that place. Ottumwa citizens favored another St. Louis–St. Paul route via Bloomfield, Ottumwa, Cedar Rapids, Waterloo, and thence over CF&M to a junction with the Minnesota Central. The management of Iowa Central had expected intrastate disharmony, but had assumed that the road's early and impressive head start plus its obvious and logical "air line" route would be adequate to forestall potential competition.[19]

Events conspired otherwise. On September 27, 1865, the St. Louis & Cedar Rapids Railway Company (StL&CR) was organized for the purpose of building a line of railroad from North Missouri's anticipated end-of-track at Coatsville, on the Iowa-Missouri border, to Cedar Rapids. There it presumably would connect with the Cedar Rapids & St. Paul Railway, chartered at about the same time. One can only guess the exact intentions of StL&CR's promoters. Some may have cared only about stopping Iowa Central. Some may have hoped to put communities such as Ottumwa and Cedar Rapids on a St. Louis–St. Paul artery. Others, like StL&CR President J. P. Farley of Dubuque County, may have wanted only to protect the interests of the river communities. Still others may have been looking out for the interests of the Chicago-based trunk roads.[20]

Iowa Central President William T. Smith initially took all of this in stride. But by the late spring of 1866, he was urging that a concerted, single effort be made to carry the Iowa Central project through to fruition. Correspondingly he counseled that it would prove disastrous for Iowans to proliferate their affections and energies; by summer there were those in Iowa and at St. Louis who agreed that it would not pay to build both Iowa Central and StL&CR. The indefatigable Smith asserted, however, that there really was room for another north-south road, but one well east of the Iowa Central, along or close to the Mississippi River. He did worry, though, that citizens of St. Louis might confuse the Iowa Central project with the StL&CR venture—a venture that he increasingly believed had been initiated solely for the purpose of killing Iowa Central. The ultimate advantage to St. Louis and to all of Iowa would be provided, he asserted, by Iowa Central—a road that would connect St. Louis with St. Paul, tap the heartland of Iowa, and cross every east-west trunk line en route. As he pointed out in a letter to the editor of the *Missouri Republican,* Chicago had "built railroads into Iowa, while your city has not a single connection of this kind in this direction, and if you do not soon secure facilities for intercourse with our people, our temporary trade will become a confirmed necessity."[21]

St. Louis journalists viewed the situation similarly. One of them, a writer for the *St. Louis Times,* predicted that completion of a road from St. Louis to the Minnesota state line would "increase the business of this city by at least one-third." The editor of the *St. Louis Republican* concurred: Iowa Central, he said, "lets St. Louis into the very heart of Iowa" and "crosses grand arterial roads by which our city will be placed in railroad connection with every portion of Iowa, and with Nebraska. It will bring Minnesota to our door."[22]

During the summer of 1867, there was apparent reassurance from the North Missouri Railroad. That road was in the process of changing its gauge from five-foot, six-inch to the standard four-foot, eight-and-a-half-inch, thus promising that cars from a northern connection could be interchanged with it. Additionally there was news that the company had 2,500 men working on its sixty-eight-mile extension from Macon to the Iowa boundary. They reportedly were laying no less than one mile of track per day. It all represented good news for Iowa Central.[23]

There was at the same time good tidings from Iowa Central itself. By July 1867, all of the grading had been completed in Black Hawk County southward from Cedar Falls, most of it had been completed in Tama County, and the entire sixty-one-mile stretch of right-of-way between Oskaloosa and the Missouri border was under contract, one-third of it already graded. The editor of the *Cedar Falls Gazette* was predictable in his support: "Be patient gentlemen, the Iowa Central is not so far in the future as you might think. Stand ready for the first trip to St. Louis." Additional good news flowed from the pen of President Smith. On May 3, he told the editor of the *St. Louis Times* that the long section between the Missouri border and Cedar

Falls would be graded and bridged by November. That same section, he continued, would be tied during the winter, and rails for it would be put down in the spring of 1868. Meanwhile, surveyors would be in the field between Cedar Falls and the Minnesota border; contracts for that section would be let in a few months. Smith asserted that with this work accomplished it would not be difficult to negotiate the road's bonds. By late summer that seemed confirmed. On September 5, 1867, the Iowa Central board met in Oskaloosa to award a contract to Champlin Balch & Co. of St. Louis—contractors associated with the North Missouri Railroad—for the swift completion of the road to Cedar Falls. That contract also provided for necessary rolling stock. The board further announced that it was negotiating for the required iron rails. Everything seemed upbeat as the year ended.[24]

Yet the passing of 1867 marked the end of good news for Iowa Central. Its promoters long had boasted that the road would be built without outside help. That proved to be an impossible dream. As early as May 1867, Iowa Central's management had asked St. Louis interests for assistance in the amount of $175,000. One booster said simply: "Money is what will complete the road." In the summer of 1868, a delegation from Iowa specifically asked citizens of St. Louis to make funds available through the Merchant's Exchange or the Board of Trade to build a bridge over the Des Moines River at Eddyville. The same delegation desperately sought assurances from North Missouri's management that when graded and tied, Iowa Central would receive the promised iron rail—and that when completed, it would, in fact, be employed as the Iowa segment of the great St. Louis–St. Paul route. The editor of the *St. Louis Republican* urged support for Iowa Central, but it was not forthcoming.[25]

Troubles suddenly multiplied. Tension developed during the spring of 1868 between Iowa

Central and Champlin Balch & Co. The contract between them—which had promised completion of the line to Cedar Falls—was dissolved. At about the same time, the Iowa legislature passed a railroad bill that allowed a tax to be levied on townships and other governmental subdivisions. It seemed to augur well for Iowa Central, but the law soon was declared unconstitutional. That proved a crushing blow, for it voided earlier commitments and precluded any assistance at all from recalcitrant Poweshiek County, where several factions long had fought for the line. Furthermore, the memorial to Congress had been given an untimely death in Washington, and potential financiers in St. Louis

began to shy away from Iowa Central. For that matter, the management of the North Missouri Railroad turned its energies to completion of another route west of Moberly that eventually linked St. Louis with Kansas City, and at the same time placed its affections in the Hawkeye State with the rival St. Louis & Cedar Rapids Railway. That road completed a line from a junction with the North Missouri Railroad at Coatsville, on the Iowa–Missouri border, to Moulton in December 1868; it would extend that line to Bloomfield in 1869, and to Ottumwa in August 1870. Because of financial problems, however, StL&CR never reached its Cedar Rapids goal, and the aspirations of North

Figure 2.3. The grade of what boosters considered "the grandest railroad project of the age," north of Toledo, never saw a train. Photograph from Ernest Sevde.

Missouri and its St. Louis sponsors in that regard were thus short-circuited.[26]

Iowa Central's death warrant was issued on June 23, 1869; it was on that day that the Central Railroad Company of Iowa (CRCI) was born. Its goal, like that of Iowa Central, was to span Iowa on a north-south axis supplying the intervening link on a St. Louis–St. Paul route. But unlike Iowa Central, CRCI represented the corporate evolution of an established operation. Its earliest predecessor, the Eldora Railroad & Coal Company, had completed a line between Ackley and Eldora in 1868.[27]

Chapter 3
ELDORA RAILROAD
& COAL COMPANY

When the Vixen *whistled some the calves stick up their tails and run.*
—*ELDORA LEDGER*, JULY 11, 1868

EARLY IN JANUARY 1866, A REPRESENTATIVE
from the firm of Edgington & Brothers
made his way to the newly opened offices
of the *Eldora Ledger.* The Edgington concern operated a daily stage line between
Iowa Falls and Marshalltown and wished to
advertise its services in the next issue and in
subsequent issues of the *Ledger.* Edgington
stages were scheduled to "leave Marshalltown
everyday on the arrival of the train from the
East, arriving at Iowa Falls on the same day. . . .
[The stages from Iowa Falls depart] everyday at
2 o'clock a.m. arriving at Marshalltown in time for
the trains going East." The route from Iowa Falls
was designed to serve the villages of Steamboat
Rock, Eldora, Union, Albion, and Marietta before making connection with the Cedar Rapids &
Missouri River Railroad (CR&MR, predecessor of
Chicago & North Western). Eldora residents were
pleased to have common carrier services afforded by
the Edgington Company, but, not unlike people in
other Midwestern communities of the post–Civil
War period, they wanted a railroad.[1]

The gently undulating prairie along the Iowa
River in central Iowa was a wild yet beckoning

wilderness when Greenberry Haggin erected
a cabin there in 1849 and thus became the
first white resident in what is now Hardin
County. By the spring of 1850, Haggin had
been joined by several other settlers, and
soon there was sufficient population to warrant the creation of a county. That was done
by an act of the General Assembly passed on
January 15, 1851.[2]

The handsome valley of the Iowa River offered
special enticements to settlers. Rich black loam was
the most appealing attraction, but almost as important was the abundant and ready supply of timber
for the construction of homes and farm buildings.
A third important asset was the rich supply of bitu-
minous coal that could be had for the taking along
the river north of what became Eldora. Indeed, this
coal was the primary factor in the rapid settlement
of the region.

As early as 1857, Captain Gustavus W. Smith
had made a survey from Dubuque to Sioux City,
noting the quality of soil and minerals between the
two points. Smith found veins of coal in the Iowa
valley to be approximately four to four and a half
feet thick and of moderately good quality. Dr. C. A.

White, the state's geologist, generally corroborated Smith's estimates, pointing out that the value of this coal was greatly enhanced because it was situated such that fuel-starved areas to the north and the west could be supplied—assuming that transportation could be arranged. Meanwhile, anybody could take what he needed from local outcroppings. As the surrounding area became increasingly populated, however, the demand for Hardin County coal grew to the point where it became profitable to exploit the resource commercially. S. A. Moran, the first coal producer, soon was joined by others in that business.[3]

Despite the well-known existence of coal in the Iowa River valley, major railroads continued to ignore Eldora. To the south, the Cedar Rapids & Missouri River Railroad was heavily engaged in its race to become the first eastern connection with Union Pacific at Council Bluffs and had little time or enthusiasm for construction of a "stub" line to tap Eldora coal banks. To the north, Dubuque & Sioux City (D&SC) had recovered from its Civil War doldrums, finally reaching Ackley on October 19, 1865, and extending services to Iowa Falls on June 1, 1866. This concern was greatly influenced by leading Dubuque personalities who certainly saw the value of spreading that city's influence to the interior of the state by means of a railway, and corporate officers of D&SC and the commercial leaders of Dubuque had been and were increasingly interested in Eldora coal—but not sufficiently to alter D&SC's projected route to tap these deposits directly. Nevertheless, far-off Dubuque would find other ways to assist Eldora in its quest for a railroad.[4]

In January 1866, the Executive Committee of the Eldora & Steamboat Rock Coal Company (the area's primary colliery) was invited to consult with Platt Smith and other Dubuque denizens for the purpose of securing aid and assistance sufficient to build a short railroad from Ackley to the mines. Dubuque & Sioux City desired Eldora coal for reve-

nue freight as well as fuel for its locomotives, but any connecting line would be corporately independent of D&SC. The Eldorans agreed to link forces with their Dubuque brethren, which resulted in the creation of the Eldora Railroad & Coal Company (ER&CC), organized for the purpose of building a railroad from Ackley to Eldora.[5]

The views of R. H. McBride, editor of the *Eldora Ledger,* were plainly colored by the presence of nearby coal. By May 1866, McBride fully sensed the importance of Eldora coal in a larger regional setting: "If this new coal company [ER&CC] will perform its part, there is no reason why the farmers on the prairies miles and miles distant should not get their coal here, for ten and fifteen cents per bushel. The day will surely come when prices like these will rule." Moreover, McBride was certain that Eldora coal, found at such a strategic location, could be marketed at competitive rates within the entire region, and eventually in remote areas—St. Paul and the aspiring communities of St. Anthony and Minneapolis, for example.[6]

The coal railroad project languished, however, until January 1867, when plans were made for a community gathering to prepare for the regular meeting of the Eldora & Steamboat Rock Coal

Figure 3.1. From this office *Eldora Ledger* editor R. H. McBride kept a close eye on railroad matters.

Company and to consider the question "Shall lands now owned by that organization be transferred to the Rail Road Company [ER&CC] when the cars run into Eldora?" McBride, of course, suggested that the community would do well to vote "Yes," urging further that "every individual who [could] possibly get out should be in attendance." The *Ledger* reminded its readers that a number of stockholders of the coal company already had agreed to the proposition. Some had given right-of-way lands. Dubuque capitalist Platt Smith promised to donate ten thousand ties to be delivered immediately at Ackley. Charles C. Gilman, president of ER&CC, was scheduled to be in attendance and would, according to McBride, give "every assurance of his sincerity, and let contracts for the road instanter." Finally, the Eldora newspaperman argued that the railroad's proposal was "no scheme, no gabble." Give an affirmative answer to this question, he said, and by the following November Eldora would be connected with the outside world.[7]

On February 5, the coal company accepted the proposals of ER&CC. Subsequently, right-of-way land and 1,300 acres in the heart of the coal fields were deeded to the railroad. In return ER&CC gave stockholders of the coal company "$30 per acre, payable in equal amounts of money, stock and bonds of the company," thereby granting considerable control of the railroad to local residents. Additionally, the railroad company agreed to "grade, tie and bridge the road from Ackley to Eldora by November 1st, 1867," but would have until July 1, 1868, to run cars into Eldora.[8]

McBride was ecstatic. Under the banner "The Dawn of a Better Day" he editorialized: "The proposed railway from Ackley to Eldora is only fifteen miles in length, but as the first link in the chain that will eventually connect Iowa and Minnesota, we hail it with rejoicing. . . . Iowa and Minnesota must be joined together before many years, and it will not be long till we can be united with St. Louis. This may be speculation today, but three years will see it well on the way to fulfillment." Perhaps his aspirations for Eldora had been sparked by a recent letter from the distant community of Albert Lea, which gave indication that Minnesota's Freeborn County was interested in the Eldora road as a possible segment in a future Minnesota–Iowa interconnection.[9]

For reasons that are not apparent, the Eldora Railroad & Coal Company suddenly found itself unable to comply with the contract as drawn, but asserted its willingness to complete the line if only the Eldora & Steamboat Rock Coal Company would "donate" the coal lands. This would save the railroad $30 per acre in stocks and bonds, but would deprive Eldora of local control. Nevertheless, the railroad was seen as a "must," and to achieve its completion a little blackmail could be tolerated. The coal company accepted the proposition, and work soon commenced on the railroad.[10]

The contract for grading, tieing, and bridging went to S. L. Dows & Company of Cedar Rapids, and carried the stipulation that work had to be completed by November 15. Sufficient stock was sold to pay the contractor for the work, and after frost had vacated the rich Iowa soil, a newly patented machine used by Dows, "The Railroad Excavator," began building roadbed. The construction company solicited ties from the immediate area, and McBride suggested that this was "a chance for some of [the local] idlers to get to work and do something." Soon 16,000 ties were on hand at Ackley.[11]

As grading progressed, the railroad company sought additional funds to purchase rolling stock and the necessary iron rail. In order to secure this capital, the company issued bonds in the amount of $400,000, secured by the usual first mortgage lien on the company's assets—the roadbed, rolling stock, lands, and mineral rights. A sufficient number of local residents, plus Dubuque investors and others, purchased these bonds so that by mid-June the *Ledger* was able to announce that delivery of iron could be expected by the end of August. Concomitantly, McBride reported, "Arrangements have gone ahead with the Illinois and Missouri Telegraph Company for the building of a line from Ackley to Eldora, to be complete by the time the cars commence running over the road."[12]

Early in July, the location for Eldora's depot was selected; according to the *Ledger,* "the locality gives general satisfaction." At the same time, there were three hundred men at work on the grade, who recently had been paid wages in the amount of $8,000. Indeed, track laying could be expected in October, and the road, in McBride's estimation, would be completed before winter. It was a bright moment. The *Ledger* offered the view that "the inventive genius of mankind has, up to this time, furnished no parallel to . . . the building of railroads across the prairies of the West." In far-off Chicago, the *Evening Journal* commended the Eldora Railroad & Coal Company for making this the first Iowa railroad to be built with local capital. It was a grand season.[13]

Clouds formed on the horizon, however, when Dubuque & Sioux City was leased to Chicago-based Illinois Central (IC) on October 1, 1867. Nevertheless, rail was being stockpiled for ER&CC at Dubuque, and by November thirteen carloads of iron had arrived at Ackley. Noting the presence of rail at Ackley and aware that the bridge over the Iowa River at Steamboat Rock was nearly complete, McBride felt that the line could yet be railed before winter if only weather conditions would remain favorable. But hope faded with the first snow flurries, and then came devastating news from Chicago: a glum Eldora learned that agreements reached earlier between the Dubuque & Sioux City and the Eldora road would not be honored by Illinois Central. There was plenty of coal in Illinois for Illinois Central's Dubuque & Sioux City locomotives, and large "eastern" carriers such as this one did not see a need to court the minuscule

interchange traffic that might derive from a yet-to-be-completed "plug" line.[14]

Construction ceased on the Eldora right-of-way; the future of the road was in grave doubt. Yet McBride's enthusiasm did not flag. In the fall of 1867, residents of Franklin and Cerro Gordo Counties to the north raised money to survey a line from Ackley all the way to Austin, Minnesota. These neighboring counties quickly pointed out that Minnesota Central, now in operation between Minneapolis/St. Paul and Owatonna, had Austin as its eventual goal, and an eighty-mile stretch was all that separated Ackley from a St. Paul connection at Austin.[15]

Meanwhile, President Gilman and Platt Smith tried unsuccessfully to lease the Eldora Railroad & Coal Company to Illinois Central. Failing in that, Gilman announced, ER&CC would consider extension of its line down the Iowa River valley to a connection with the Cedar Rapids & Missouri River Railroad at or near Marshalltown. Completion of the line from Ackley to Eldora plus new construction to link Eldora and Marshalltown would afford residents of Hardin County outlet to two strong east-west carriers and thereby negate the problems of monopoly that came with single-option routings. Besides, there was the possibility that CR&MR might be enticed to lease the entire ER&CC.[16]

By mid-April 1868, cars of the Eldora road were making regular trips, with several shipments of potatoes, corn, and coal moving out of the Steamboat Rock railhead northward to Ackley. By this time rails had been thrust south about one mile beyond the Iowa River in order to serve the coal mines, and the depot at Steamboat Rock was nearly completed.[17]

Meanwhile, President Charles C. Gilman was in New York to promote the sale of Eldora Railroad & Coal Company securities. Readers of the ER&CC prospectus that Gilman was distributing undoubtedly noted the heavy emphasis that he placed on the Hardin County coal deposits: "In quality, this coal does not vary materially from that of Illinois or in other parts of Iowa, possessing this remarkable characteristic, however, which makes it valuable for

fuel purposes in burning to ashes without fusing or 'clinkering.'" Before returning to Iowa, Gilman arranged to "purchase passenger cars, locomotive and other equipment, absolutely called for by the increased business on the Eldora Railroad." Business on the local road *was* good, with heavy shipments of wheat, corn, potatoes, fire clay, and coal moving daily from Steamboat Rock to the junction at Ackley.[18]

Illinois Central's D&SC quite clearly was willing to handle traffic to and from the "Plug," but the larger road had little interest in owning or leasing the line. Rebuffed by IC and fearful of the difficulties inherent in any single-line connection, the management of the Eldora Railroad & Coal Company came to grips with reality—it was necessary to expand or wither. Surveys had been made earlier in a northerly direction from Ackley, but President Gilman now looked to the south and in the late spring of 1868 made a firm commitment to finish the "Plug" into Eldora, thence continuing down the Iowa River valley to connection with Chicago & North Western's Cedar Rapids & Missouri River Railroad. Extension of the Eldora road southward to CR&MR would have immediate short-range benefits, he had decided, while a connection with the markets of neighboring Minnesota held long-range possibilities.[19]

Currently the "Plug" was performing acceptably in its own right. Receipts for the line were averaging $300 per day, and McBride opined that this was

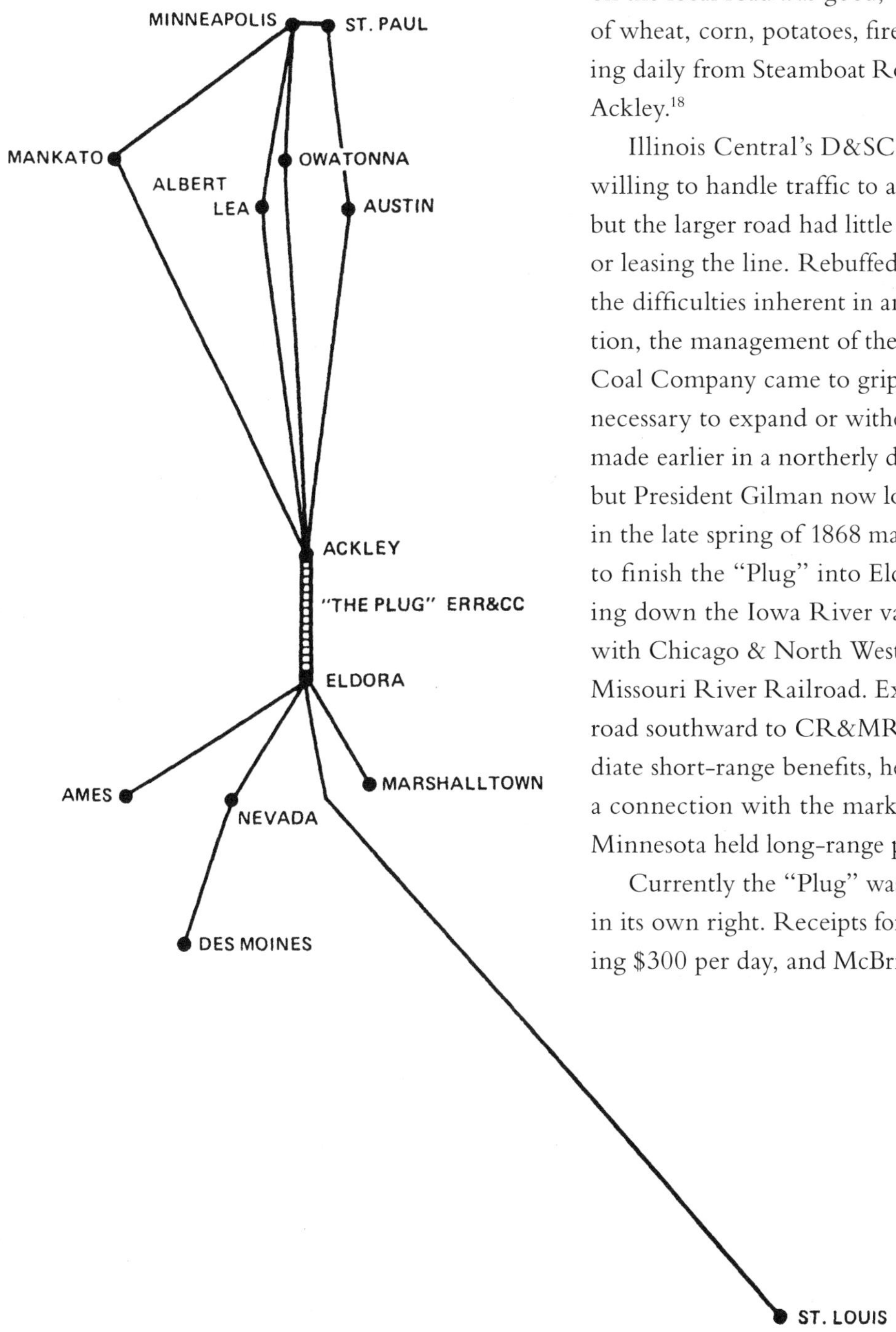

Map 3.1. This map suggests that the location of Eldora and Hardin County was such as to make them the hub of a transportation wheel.

"mighty clever for a young railroad only twelve miles long." Perhaps the bulk of credit for the road's performance was due to President Charles Gilman—"at no distant day, if not already, destined to be the foremost of the leading men of Iowa," as the *Cedar Falls Gazette* predicted—who increasingly sought to control the road by buying out the original investors. Gilman purchased a home in Eldora and soon moved his family to Hardin County.[20]

From the time the Eldora road had opened for business, its sole locomotive had been the *Vixen,* "a light draft engine given to sparking considerably." By the spring of 1868, the volume of business had increased to the point where Gilman had the pleasant task of ordering a "large sized powerful engine; . . . a jewel . . . worthy to sound its throat on the beautiful prairies of Iowa." Moreover, Gilman announced that work would commence at once on the grade between the mines and Eldora. With ties down, rails would not be long in arriving. Plans also went forward to build a depot at Ackley near the junction of the "Plug" and Illinois Central.[21]

President Gilman was serious about extending the road from Eldora down the Iowa River valley to CR&MR, but he had never clearly indicated that Marshalltown was the company's ultimate goal. That kind of deceptiveness often was employed by railroad promoters of the period, and the implications were not lost on communities aspiring to receive initial or additional rail service. Should Gilman build his road to a point on CR&MR some few miles west of the Marshall County seat, it was clear that Marshalltown's future would be seriously endangered. Gilman allowed the seeds of this implied threat to germinate in the minds of the Marshalltown citizenry, and not surprisingly a letter soon came from a leading resident of that city who urged Gilman to build the line by way of Marshalltown. The railroad president responded by saying that his company was anxious to extend the road and would do so immediately "if sufficient encouragement were given by the people along the line." Gilman was practicing the classic form of railroad bribery; Marshalltown knew it, but the outcome remained in doubt.[22]

Meanwhile, the Eldora road offered two regularly scheduled trips per day from Steamboat Rock, "making close connections at Ackley with East and West trains of the D&SCRR." These trains returned to Steamboat Rock and there connected with stages for Eldora, Albion, and Marshalltown. Stagecoach service between Eldora and Steamboat Rock was augmented by a "hack line of omnibuses" operated by B. E. Deyo.[23]

Arrival of the "iron horse" at Eldora was imminent, however, and each new development brought much excitement along the Iowa River valley. In June, McBride reported that construction on the two-story, thirty-by-seventy-foot depot at Eldora was progressing nicely; he contended that it would be the "nicest depot" between the Iowa and Mississippi Rivers. At the same time the "Plug" took delivery of "a new and splendid passenger and baggage car" with patent ventilation and green enameled cushions, recently outshopped by Jackson & Sharpe of Wilmington, Delaware.[24]

With the arrival of the new passenger car, Eldorans were promised an excursion on the Fourth of July. McBride heralded the event with the banner headline "Good Time Coming," and counseled readers to "prepare their good clothes for a grand jubilee and excursion July next. [Local residents will] . . . have a free ride over the Eldora Railroad, and in that Company's passenger cars." Charles Gilman was appreciative of the fine cooperation that Eldorans had given his enterprise; it was fitting that he repay the compliment by providing an excursion over the new road—and its Ackley connection as well. Soon the project mushroomed into the social event of the season, perhaps the decade. Arrangements were made with Dubuque & Sioux City to handle the excursion train over its line from

Ackley to Cedar Falls and then north on D&SC's
Cedar Falls & Minnesota to Nashua. Inasmuch as
rails had not yet arrived in Eldora, the excursion
would begin at Steamboat Rock. Departure time
for the "Special" was set at 7:00 a.m., with the
return to be at 8:00 p.m. Earlier indications that
the excursion would be "free" had hinged on the
notion that the excursion train would operate solely
over rails of the Eldora Road. In order to afford
the ambitious outing over D&SC rails to Nashua,
however, Gilman reluctantly agreed that it would
be necessary to charge every excursionist $1 for the
round trip.[25]

The *Eldora Ledger* of July 11 carried McBride's
flowery description of the tour to Nashua. On
the great day, the depot at Steamboat Rock had
thronged with people who had begun arriving at
dawn. Soon Engineer Vedder sounded the whistle
of the *Vixen,* and the grand entourage made its way
up the short but steep grade leading out of the Iowa
River valley onto the lush prairie for its twelve-
mile run to Ackley. The country along the route
of the Eldora road was typical of the best farmland in Iowa, and the excursionists undoubtedly
took pride in viewing this rich panorama. After
a "thirty minute flight" the train pulled to a stop
at Ackley, where Eldora cars were added to those
owned by D&SC. It was a lengthy train, carrying
approximately 1,500 excursionists. The Eldora cars,
including "the handsome coach just received by the
Eldora R.R., led the van, while green boughs and
small flags fluttered and waved over all."[26]

The return trip found a number of excursionists in a reflective if festive mood. It was generally
concluded among them that Charles C. Gilman,
whom McBride described as "not good looking"
but a "western working man," had been responsible
for the arrival of the steamcars along the Iowa River
valley. In one of the coaches a group of men had
fortified their general ebullience with corn whiskey,

and as they considered Gilman's contributions one
of their number concocted the following:

Here's a health to President Gilman,
Drink it down.
That's his "plug," we now can scan,
Drink it down.
For if you want some railroads,
He's the boy to build 'em.
Drink it down, drink it down, drink it down.

It was almost dark when D&SC delivered the
Eldora cars to Gilman's road at Ackley. Shortly
thereafter the *Vixen* had the "home" cars in tow.[27]

The Nashua Fourth of July outing was a tre-
mendous success. Gilman had provided area
residents with extremely pleasant memories, but,
more important, at Nashua he had taken the opportunity to confirm the rumor that a number of
corporate changes soon would take place. Simply
stated, the Eldora Railroad & Coal Company was
to be dissolved, with its railroad operations to be
assumed by the new Iowa River Railway and its
mining operations to be retained by the Eldora
Coal Company. The Iowa River Railway, Gilman
announced, would authorize construction of a road
from Eldora south to CR&MR. Beyond junction
with the Cedar Rapids road, however, the Iowa
River Railway projected a line of construction
"following down the sixteenth meridian of longitude to the Missouri state line," where it planned
to effect a junction with a St. Louis company.
Meanwhile, production of coal from the Eldora
banks was increasing, and McBride predicted an
output of five hundred tons per day during the
coming winter season.[28]

Shortly after the Fourth of July, tracklaying
began along the line from the coal mines southward to Eldora, and on July 18 McBride eagerly
announced that the rails were within two and a half
miles of town. During the last week of July, Eldora
became a railroad town *and* the permanent county

seat—all on the same day. Almost simultaneously with the arrival of the construction crew came a messenger from Des Moines with news that the Iowa Supreme Court had resolved lengthy litigation regarding the location of the county seat in favor of Eldora. Celebrations to herald the arrival of the "iron horse" had been scheduled at the depot; these festivities were carried out forthwith, while another celebration was held at the courthouse. Bonfires burned until midnight, a "salute of 100 guns was fired, . . . speeches were made by those not too full of utterance, 'and all went merry as a marriage bell.'" On hand for the driving of the last spike was President Charles Gilman, along with Horace Abbott, Thomas Kensett, and Jonathan Gilman, the latter three Baltimore capitalists. These men had become closely associated with the new Iowa River Railway and would greatly assist Gilman and local supporters in a quest for "foreign" capital that was essential if the line was to be extended.[29]

By August 10, agent John Gilman, formerly company representative at Steamboat Rock, accepted the first freight shipment at Eldora when John Findley sent several cars of cattle to market. Business flourished at the new railhead, and shortly the company took receipt of twelve new boxcars, which immediately were pressed into service. The new locomotive ordered earlier to handle the in-creasing traffic arrived on August 20. Christened *Thomas Kensett,* this beautiful twenty-six-and-one-half-ton coal burner had come directly from the East Boston shops of McKay & Aldus and was the pride of the road. Construction of the Eldora depot had been completed by a Dubuque contractor, who now labored at the installation of a forty-five-foot turntable, an important symbol of permanence. Indeed, Charles Gilman announced that the headquarters of the Iowa River Railway would remain in Hardin County, where he could properly direct the operations of the railroad while at the same time exercising his presidency of the Eldora Coal Mining Company.[30]

As summer faded into fall, freight and passenger traffic steadily increased. Coal was moving well, agricultural products were shipped daily, inbound merchandise traffic was good, and passenger volume mushroomed. The daily (except Sunday) schedule for September 1868 included two round-trips to Ackley. Passengers and freight were handled on all trains. Connection was made at Ackley with Illinois Central trains and at Eldora with Marshalltown stages. In Eldora, B. E. Deyo, owner of the Eastern House, a hotel, operated a free omnibus to and from the railroad station. Modern life truly had come to the seat of Hardin County.[31]

Chapter 4
IOWA RIVER RAILWAY

These bonds, though not bearing a very high interest rate,
are paying as much as any legitimate operation can afford to—a point to be considered
in the minds of those who seek a secure and safe investment.
—A. L. HATCH, NEW YORK BOND AGENT, REFERRING TO PROSPECTS FOR THE IOWA RIVER RAILWAY

CHARLES CARROLL GILMAN, PRESIDENT OF the newly formed Iowa River Railway, was born on February 22, 1833, the son of Doctor and Mrs. Gilman, residents of Brooks, Maine. Young Gilman attended Waterville College in Maine and then studied medicine with his father. When his health failed, the future Iowa railroad president sought recovery in strenuous out-of-doors work. After a brief stay in Michigan, he continued west to Iowa, arriving at Dubuque in 1857. While a resident of that eastern Iowa community, Gilman engaged in the wholesale lumber trade and eventually opened retail yards in many surrounding towns. Later he was responsible for the founding of Earlville, became active in the grain business, dabbled with farming in Delaware County, and erected flour and sawmills at Hillsdale. In 1864, he campaigned for federal funds to be used in the removal of rapids that encumbered water transportation on the Mississippi River between Keokuk and Davenport. During 1865, he was one of a number of businessmen who founded the Dubuque Produce Exchange. The following year, he and other Dubuque civic leaders labored for completion of a

rail bridge over the Mississippi River linking the Dubuque & Sioux City Railroad on the Iowa side with Illinois Central on the eastern bank. Through service to Chicago was initiated on January 1, 1869, when the bridge was formally opened for traffic.[1]

About the time construction crews started driving piling for the Mississippi bridge, Gilman became more and more engrossed with his responsibilities for the Eldora Railroad & Coal Company, and in 1867 he decided to move his home to Eldora from Dubuque. Although business interests were to carry him away from Eldora periodically, that central Iowa town was to be his home for as long as he lived.

The Eldora company had received a severe setback, of course, when Illinois Central had voided the contract between the Eldora Railroad & Coal Company and the Dubuque & Sioux City Railroad. Consequently, ER&CC had suffered uneasy moments and might well have suffered Iowa's first railroad abandonment had it not been for the efforts of its energetic president. Charles Gilman fortunately had several influential friends, and he turned to them for financial aid. F. W. H. Sheffield of

23

Figure 4.1. Charles Carroll Gilman headed the Eldora Railroad & Coal Company and then the Iowa River Railway.

Dubuque as well as A. H. Hatch and H. P. Liscomb of New York were persuaded to help Gilman when he suggested that they give him sufficient funds to buy out all other parties identified with the Eldora Railroad & Coal Company. They did this, and Gilman worked quickly to write up the "Articles of Incorporation of the Iowa River Railroad Company." These were filed for the record on July 8, 1868.[2]

The new company had as its dual purposes acquisition of the Eldora company and lengthening of its route from Eldora south to a connection with the Cedar Rapids & Missouri River Railroad. Gilman executed an exchange agreement whereby the new company issued $270,000 in first mortgage bonds and $510,000 in stock for the properties of the Eldora road. Furthermore, Gilman agreed to

issue another $90,000 in stock, payable to owners of the Eldora Railroad & Coal Company when the Iowa River Railway was completed to a proposed junction with CR&MR.[3]

The Iowa River Railway was authorized to issue a maximum capital stock of $7 million, but this was not to exceed $30,000 per mile of road graded and tied. Moreover, the stock was to be issued only as fast as the road was ready for rail. The company also was authorized to issue bonds up to $16,000 per mile of road ready for single-track operation. The headquarters of the new company was to be located at Eldora, and plans were made to build a roundhouse at that point. The first board of directors consisted of C. C. Gilman of Eldora; Wells S. Riche of Marshalltown; F. W. H. Sheffield of Dubuque; Horace Abbott, Thomas Kensett, and Jonathan S. Gilman of Baltimore; and Isaac Hyde Jr. of New York. C. C. Gilman was elected president, Thomas Kensett vice president.[4]

The Eldora Railroad & Coal Company had been, in effect, split into two separate entities. The coal mining operations were reorganized as the Eldora Coal Mining Company, and the rail operations were conveyed by Gilman to the Iowa River Railway. The new road had a contract with the coal company, starting January 1, 1869, which called for one hundred tons of coal per day, "to be increased as demand along the line may require," but each operation was to be independent of the other.[5]

Gilman's immediate task was to spike down rails leading to the Cedar Rapids & Missouri River connection "at or near Marshalltown." Marshalltown (the name of which had been changed from Marshall on May 5, 1863) already was basking in the luxury of an east-west trunk line and, though passively interested in the adventures of Gilman, was smug in its assumption that should Gilman, in fact, push his rails to CR&MR, he would most certainly choose Marshalltown as the junction point. Therefore, it was with surprise and great distress that Marshalltown residents learned that Iowa River engineers had surveyed south from Eldora along the banks of the river, leaving the bottoms to pass through Marietta and greet the Cedar Rapids road southwest of Marshalltown.[6]

Meanwhile, the Iowa General Assembly recently had succumbed to a bout of railroad fever, passing a law authorizing townships to vote taxes up to 5 percent in aid of railroad construction. Residents of Hardin County earlier had given land for right-of-way and certain coal fields to promote ER&CC, but Marshall County townships, reluctant in the beginning, only now voted aid for Iowa River Railway in the amount of $80,000, with certain additional benefits to be paid "on condition of the road being built." Gilman returned the compliment by ordering his engineers to make a revised survey designed to take the road directly down the valley to Marshalltown. Twenty-seven miles, from Eldora to Marshalltown, was put under contract in October 1868, and grading was about half finished before cold weather put a stop to operations.[7]

Winter also provided Gilman with time for reflection as to the ultimate future of the enterprise. His efforts not surprisingly had served to revive hopes for a north-south railroad cutting across the heart of Iowa, connecting St. Paul with St. Louis, especially because the Iowa Central Railroad was at a standstill east of Eldora and prospects for its completion were bleak indeed. Meanwhile, the North Missouri Railroad stood as a "lady-in-waiting" at the Iowa–Missouri border, while at the same time Minnesota railroads were working south toward Iowa. The company's board of directors ultimately concurred with Gilman's recommendation to push the road to both the northern and the southern borders of Iowa, but of course the immediate goals of the Iowa River Railway were to gain a connection with CR&MR and to maintain operation of the former Eldora road north to Ackley. They thought the next season, 1869, should see the road safely into Marshalltown, however, and then its promoters could devote their entire energies to the "avowed

purpose of constructing and maintaining a North and South line of railway through the central portion of the State of Iowa from the Southern boundary line of Minnesota to the Northern boundary of Missouri, a distance of 250 miles."[8]

By striking down the sixteenth degree of longitude, or as near thereto as practicable, the proposed line would traverse some of the richest and best settled agricultural and mineral districts of Iowa. Furthermore, such a route would integrate already completed trackage as well as that currently under construction. By building north from Ackley to Hampton, skirting the east side of Clear Lake, and crossing the Iowa-Minnesota boundary in the northeast corner of Winnebago County, a through route to St. Paul could be effected in conjunction with the Minnesota Valley Railroad (Chicago & North Western's predecessor) at Mankato. In order to connect with the North Missouri Railroad, a line would have to be built south from Marshalltown to strike the Missouri border somewhere near the middle of Davis County. Such a line, Gilman thought, should be built via Grinnell, Oskaloosa, and Eddyville and on through Wapello and Davis Counties. This was indeed an energetic plan, far removed from the original notion of merely moving Hardin County coal to the Dubuque & Sioux City Railroad at Ackley. Gilman, however, was an energetic and enterprising man. This project was not beyond his capabilities—if money could be raised.[9]

The Iowa River Railway's prospectus sounded very much like a rehash of arguments that Iowa Central Railroad promoters had used to solicit support for their road. The authors of the Iowa River prospectus spoke in glowing terms of possibilities for moving grain from the region, but really warmed to their task when they came to prospects for coal traffic, noting that the coal around Eldora as well as that in Mahaska County could be easily mined and would be in great demand "far and wide." Grain traffic was inherent to any Midwest railroad, but coal—and this coal was "superior in quality"—was not readily available to most roads and to the communities that they might serve. Surely there would be an insatiable demand for this fuel, and, moreover, the known supply in these two regions was practically unlimited. The Mahaska veins were "from four to nine feet in thickness," the Eldora beds slightly less abundant.[10]

Generous traffic in grains and coal would fatten the coffers of any railroad, but an additional asset of the proposed north-south line would be the lumber traffic that certainly would move over it, because the available timber supply in Iowa and in surrounding states was practically negligible. Pineries of the North were then shipping their production to southern destinations via Chicago, but this costly routing could easily be obviated by a direct path south from St. Paul and Minneapolis gateways. Grain, coal, and lumber would be the mainstays of the proposed cross-Iowa line, and, coupled with general passenger and freight traffic, these would yield volumes adequate to put a smile on the face of any company treasurer. Finally, a St. Louis gateway was patently desirable because Iowa customers presently were forced to deal mostly with Chicago merchants, resulting in "an unjust monopoly." Iowa would enjoy a competitive market only if St. Louis could be reached by a direct all-weather route such as that proposed by the Iowa River Railway. As an aside, the authors of the company's prospectus noted that the proposed line would cross several east-west roads, affording any number of alternate and competitive routes for any remaining Chicago traffic.[11]

When the Iowa River Railway acquired ER&CC on September 1, 1868, the new owners gained seventeen miles of track built by the Eldora company as well as two depot buildings (at Steamboat Rock and Eldora), a coal house, two turntables, and two track scales. In addition, rolling stock in the form of "one new twenty-six ton locomotive, twenty freight cars, one passenger and baggage car . . . and four hand cars" came to Iowa

River. To these Gilman added a new thirty-ton locomotive and twelve new boxcars.[12]

On the first day of 1869, Gilman informed the board of directors that the new equipment plus that acquired from ER&CC would be sufficient to operate the present line. The road was, however, in the midst of expansion toward Marshalltown and would need additional expenditures during the next year. Gilman suggested as necessary for this extension, among other things, station houses at Abbott, Union, Norris, Albion, and Marshalltown—and, of course, forty-four miles of telegraph line.[13]

If the road's investors were curious as to whether the young line would be a moneymaker, general freight agent J. W. Gilman thought he had the answer, noting that for the last four months of 1868 (since the acquisition of the Eldora Company) the road had had gross earnings amounting to $14,470.25 against operating expenses totaling $6,575.28. Furthermore, it had paid interest on the January coupons ($7,893.00). J. W. Gilman admitted that passenger and express revenues accounted for only $2,677.55 of the total, but after all, he pointed out, the Iowa River Railway had not been designed to be an important passenger carrier.[14]

Winter passed quickly, and Iowa River's enthusiastic management eagerly looked forward to spring and the beginning of their final thrust toward the Marshall County seat. As the immediate goal of reaching Marshalltown was almost certain at this juncture, however, Gilman and his lieutenants made further long range plans designed to ensure the building of the road to the Minnesota and Missouri borders.

Earnest discussion likely focused on which directional goal ought to be given priority. Should the road first vent its energies toward procurement of northern connections, or should it head south toward the North Missouri Railroad? A decision was not long in coming, for news reached the Iowa River management that a rival concern, the Iowa & Minnesota Railroad, had announced intentions of building a line northward from Des Moines, paralleling the Iowa River Railway and about eighteen miles distant. Gilman was galvanized into action by this news; the question as to which direction should receive priority had been settled in favor of the north.[15]

The Iowa River Railway had an advantage over its prospective competitor because it already had mileage in operation and more in the construction stage. Gilman advised the company's board members that they should push their advantage by establishing another company called the St. Louis & St. Paul Railroad. Agreement came quickly. This new road was to issue no bonds or stock, but was charged with the responsibility of grading a line north from Ackley to the Minnesota state line. The route was to be "via Hampton."[16]

Simultaneously, the directors sought to cover the road's southern flank by immediately starting negotiations with the beleaguered directors of the now nearly defunct Iowa Central Railroad. That company, of course, had graded several miles of line in southern Iowa that could be used by the Iowa River road. Gilman had previously acknowledged an interest in the Iowa Central, but now action seemed imperative.

Meanwhile, contractors finished their work on the Iowa River grade, and track gangs spiked down rail after rail on their trek from Eldora toward Marshalltown. To the north, St. Louis & St. Paul agents were busy contracting with construction companies and farmers along the proposed route for the use of men, horses, scrapers, and other machinery and tools that would be needed to throw up a grade north from Ackley. It was a busy time for Gilman and the board, for they were actively completing plans for yet another new railroad company.

Chapter 5
CENTRAL RAILROAD COMPANY OF IOWA

A telegraph wire was attached to the polished spike and another wrapped around the hammer which was to send it home, so that the electric circle was made complete when the hammer rested on the spike. Each tap was heard by friends in New York.
—J. M. CHAMBERLAIN, REPORTING ON COMPLETION OF THE CENTRAL'S CONSTRUCTION BETWEEN SEARSBORO AND NEW SHARON ON FEBRUARY 4, 1871

ON JUNE 23, 1869, INCORPORATORS OF THE Central Railroad Company of Iowa (CRCI or the Central) met at Marshalltown to affix their signatures to that new firm's articles of incorporation. The Central's objectives were practically the same as those of the Iowa River Railway, except that the new road announced that points on the "old" Iowa Central had been "established." What this meant, in fact, was that Gilman had been successful in negotiating an agreement whereby the "property, rights, and franchises of . . . the . . . Iowa Central Railroad Company . . . about sixty five miles of line . . . [had been] acquired by purchase." President Gilman earlier had concluded that the portion of Iowa Central grade running south from near Oskaloosa would fit into his plans for expansion toward the North Missouri Railroad, and it was this section that CRCI had procured. The matter was not entirely completed, however, until June 1870, when the Iowa River Railway Company, the St. Louis & St. Paul Railroad, and the "old" Iowa Central Railroad were consolidated.[1]

Gilman arranged for a $4 million loan from the Farmers Loan & Trust of New York on July 15, 1869. This was granted on the security of "a thirty

year mortgage or deed of trust from the Central Railroad Company of Iowa." Money for construction was immediately available from the operating revenue of the Iowa River Railway, the sale of stocks and bonds, and this newly consummated agreement with the Farmers Loan company.[2]

Gilman, who earlier had been elected president of the new road, was active on three fronts at once. He hurried grading contractors on the route north of Ackley (the St. Louis & St. Paul section); he ordered crews to work on the grade in southern Iowa; and, most especially, he directed his energies toward finally getting rails into Marshalltown—which the Central had prudently selected as its principal place of business.[3]

The road's management was still undecided as to which tack the road should take upon reaching Hampton, sixteen miles north of Ackley. Plans had called for the Iowa River Railway to push northwestward toward Mankato, Minnesota. Now, however, the Central seemed disposed to build its line toward the Milwaukee & St. Paul (successor to the Minnesota Central and a Milwaukee predecessor), which had completed a line from St. Paul to Austin, twelve miles north of the Iowa border. The revised route would see the Central operating via Nora Springs to a junction with the Milwaukee & St. Paul at the state line in Mitchell County. Final plans, however, were not required until rails were pushed into Hampton.

To hurry the line toward eventual St. Paul–St. Louis connections, Gilman and local promoters had been forced to make vigorous appeals to Eastern capitalists. They did not look with favor on losing control to Eastern investment bankers, but they understood that gaining capital was mandatory if their company was to fill the gap between north and south.

While notables such as Jay Cooke and J. Edgar Thomson were now numbered among the large stockholders of the Iowa road, Gilman could take pride in the fact that Iowa retained considerable influence on the board of directors. Gilman was president, of course, and a board member as well. He was joined by R. W. H. Sheffield, president of the Merchants National Bank of Dubuque; G. M. Woodbury, president of the First National Bank of Marshalltown; Josiah B. Grinnell, president of the First National Bank of Grinnell; and W. H. Seevers of Oskaloosa, who also acted as the road's vice president. The vast majority of the stock was controlled, however, by the remaining members of the board—W. A. Wheelock, president of the Central National Bank of New York; J. J. Donaldson, president of the Bank of North America in New York; W. B. Shattuck (the road's treasurer) of New York; John S. Gilman, president of the Second National Bank of Baltimore; Thomas Kensett of Baltimore; and Horace Abbott of the Abbott Iron Works in Baltimore.[4]

It must have galled the energetic Gilman to be forced to solicit advice from Eastern members of the board. For that matter, Gilman was out of character anytime he solicited advice. Heretofore he had moved with near abandon. Now he was obliged to answer to a number of "foreign" men on the board, to the Farmers Loan & Trust Company,

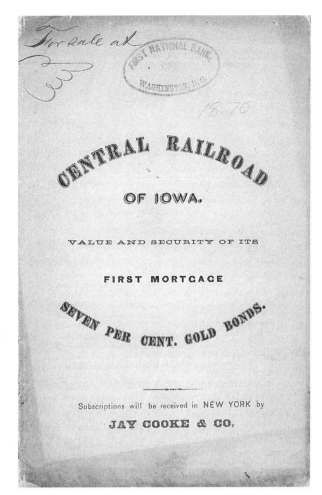

Figure 5.1. Jay Cooke & Company actively solicited sales of Central's securities and also acquired its own stake in the Iowa road.

and to various bondholders. It was this latter group that had stipulated that, in case the road defaulted on its semiannual bond interest, the majority of bondholders would attach the property and/or sell it at auction to the highest bidder. The pressure was on. Gilman, who now labored as general superintendent as well as president of the road, had the responsibility not only of building the line, but also of operating it—at a profit.[5]

The original progress estimates of the Iowa River engineers proved to be overly optimistic. As the first frost of the season signaled the approach of winter, track gangs still toiled to get rails into Marshalltown. Adverse weather was the primary culprit behind multitudinous delays. Persistence finally paid off in December, however, when construction was finished on the Eldora–Marshalltown segment. Surfacing remained to be done, but the line was finally opened to service on January 7, 1870, giving rise to "great rejoicing by the people." Marshalltown now boasted of a mainline east-west railroad and a productive independent feeder from the north.[6]

With the opening of the line to Marshalltown, the Central operated 54.22 miles of trackage and enjoyed an expansive interchange with two major east-west trunk lines. Its promoters in the East—among them Jay Cooke, the Bank of North America, and Howes & Macy—now could announce the road's progress as well as its proposals for future construction. The sale of bonds was proceeding nicely, and with a robust national economy the total issue would soon be placed.

Winter afforded a brief respite for the graders and track gangs. It also afforded Eastern representatives another opportunity to advertise the Central's bonds. Sales personnel noted that several hundred thousand dollars' worth had been sold already, and pointed out that the region traversed by the Central was "known to be the garden of the state." W. B. Shattuck, the road's treasurer, argued that the securities offered were indeed safe and that he had made a "careful personal investigation of the line." He pointed out repeatedly that "Western roads" were earning a handsome return for their owners and that preliminary information suggested that it might be possible for the Iowa company to earn as much as $9,000 per mile per annum, but "if only one half of this sum is earned, the interest is [still] perfectly secure." And the treasurer reminded prospective purchasers that the road was bonded at only $16,000 per mile.[7]

By March of 1870, Minnesota Central was able to announce that 117 miles of its railroad between St. Paul and Austin, Minnesota, was in operation. At the same time, the St. Paul & Sioux City Railroad planned to construct its line south-

westward from Mankato to the Iowa border. The Gilman management had, by this time, fully determined to use the bulk of its energies to build CRCI to a junction with Milwaukee & St. Paul, but it also considered an outlet to the north via St. Paul & Sioux City. Furthermore, Gilman knew that another Minnesota concern was planning a line southward from Minneapolis. This road, styled the Minnesota Western Railroad Company, was a predecessor of the Minneapolis & St. Louis (M&StL).[8]

Meanwhile, work had gone forward on the grade to Hampton and beyond, and twenty-three miles of it was ready for rail before the St. Louis & St. Paul and its parent, the Iowa River Railroad, both were absorbed by the Central.[9]

By the time grading was resumed in the spring of 1870, the Central's management had fully decided to build the company's line from Hampton to Mason City—as opposed to all other alternatives. The basis of this decision centered on the fact that both St. Paul & Sioux City Railroad and M&StL could easily build their respective lines to Mason City should they truly wish to secure junction with the Central. Further, CRCI management felt that a connection with Milwaukee & St. Paul could readily be effected if the Central itself were to build a branch northeastward from Mason City to the St. Paul's end-of-tracks at the Minnesota state line. Finally, the Central's management was fully aware that both Mason City and Cerro Gordo County had happily voted a 5 percent levy, the proceeds of which were to be given to the Central upon completion of its line to the seat of Cerro Gordo County.

By June 1870, President Gilman was able to report "that about three thousand men [were] now at work." The fruits of their labors were manifest; the "iron horse" pushed into Hampton on Tuesday, June 28, 1870.[10]

In a day when procurement of a rail line was the foremost goal of any Midwestern community, Hampton "formally" received the Central on the

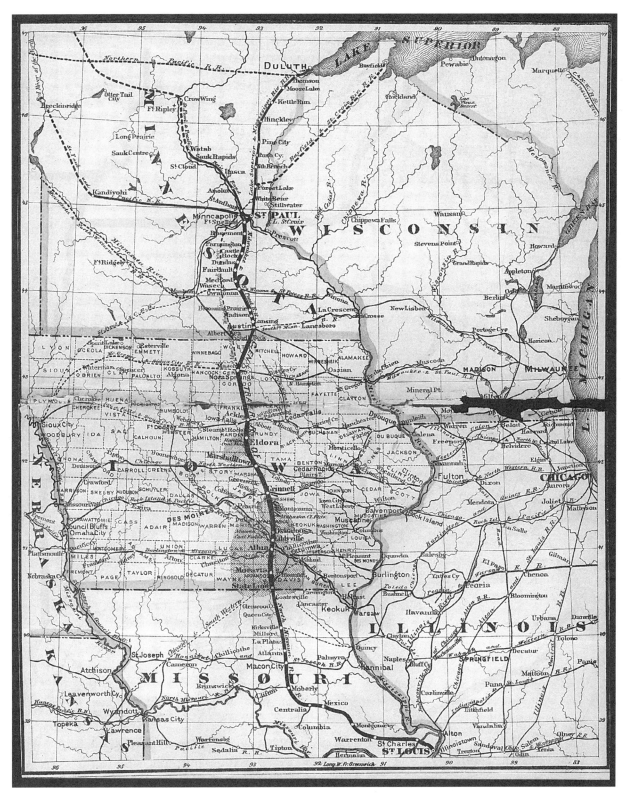

Map 5.1. This map shows Central's lines as well as its principal connections and aspirations.

Fourth of July, 1870. A celebration on that date had been traditional at Hampton, and President Gilman advised the town fathers that for this one the Central would assist by bringing in a train bearing two thousand excursionists. As one writer later recalled, the town planned to put its "best foot forward on that day and have such a celebration as would put all previous efforts to shame and make surrounding towns hang their heads with envy." The following is a description of what happened:

> The eventful day dawned bright and clear and public expectation was at the highest pitch. Hampton for the first time was to show herself to the world as a railroad town. The train came in from the south about half past ten. All Hampton was at the depot. It turned out to be only a "special" bearing President Gilman and a few of his friends. They did not disembark, but after a few moments delay backed out of town. Still, we stand, waiting for the other special with "at least 2,000 people." At noon it came, with fifteen to sixteen flat cars with bushes stuck in the sides for shade.
>
> The afternoon was pandemonium let loose. A large number of the track-laying gang of the railroad were here, and while the crowd that came on the excursion from the south were mainly respectable people, there was a sprinkling of "toughs" among them. (We had a few of those in our town here in those days, too.) There was a "blind pig" near the depot where whiskey was freely dispensed. And somehow or other there were other supplies of the same class of goods in town. We had no city marshal, and as the afternoon wore away the crowd became more uproarious and disorderly. The Fourth of July marshall [sic] undertook at one time to stop a row, but he speedily abandoned the job and got out of sight, nor by the way, was

> he ever seen subsequently, as he evacuated the town, with all his belongings, before daylight the next morning.
>
> Luckily no damage was done, except a few windows broken and a few heads slightly cracked, all casualties being among those engaged in the fun. But it was a long time before you could mention that Fourth of July celebration in this town without the man addressed would either swear or laugh, accordingly as he had been personally interested in the occasion.[11]

In June President Gilman had announced, "We now have no reason to doubt that the entire line will be finished this year." Indeed the work was being "vigorously pushed." Crews drove track into Mason City during November 1870. Mason City was happy to receive this north-south connection, of course, and had gladly subscribed to aid building of the line, but the glamor of receiving a railroad had worn off after the McGregor & Missouri River (still another Milwaukee predecessor) had arrived a year earlier, on November 7, 1869. Thus no big celebration was staged for the Central's arrival.[12]

Meanwhile, at about the same time an agreement was made whereby "the 28 miles from the Minnesota line to Mason City . . . [were to be] . . . laid under mutual and favorable arrangements, by the Milwaukee & St. Paul Railroad Company." Accordingly, in 1870 Milwaukee & St. Paul authorized—under the watchful eye of Russell Sage, the "Money King"—organization of the Mason City & Minnesota Railway for the purpose of building a line from Lyle, south of Austin on the Minnesota border, to Mason City, twenty-eight miles away. That task was completed just as the Central was pushing its rails in from the south; in that way Mason City & Minnesota met its parent, Milwaukee & St. Paul, at Lyle, and by an interchange of cars afforded the Central a much-desired connection to and from St. Paul. The junction with the Milwaukee & St. Paul lines at Mason City initiated a working relationship that was to last for many years.[13]

Even as track gangs were busy driving the line northward, a number of crews were building a line from Marshalltown south to the "old" Iowa Central grade near Oskaloosa. The Burlington & Missouri River Railroad had reached Albia, the capital of Monroe County, in 1866, but the populace there, while thrilled to have been chosen to receive this important east-west road, also desired a north-south line. To this end, they joined with residents of nearby Monroe County townships to vote aid in the amount of $100,000 for construction of the line—provided, of course, that it was in fact built from Oskaloosa to Albia. Additional inducement took another form: many prosperous coal mines would be tapped by the new road, and traffic from those mines would immediately yield very welcome revenue. Indeed, Milwaukee & St. Paul, CRCI's connection at Mason City, would soon operate over one thousand miles of track, and as quickly as southern Iowa coal was available that road would be in the market for vast quantities to be used as locomotive fuel.[14]

Gilman weighed the advantages of a route through Albia against the benefits of a more direct survey to the Iowa-Missouri state line. He chose the Albia proposition. In either case, he noted, it would be possible to use a large part of the "old" Iowa Central grade south of Oskaloosa. A "jog" could be made into Albia, and by projecting the line southeastward from that place, the old Central grade could be regained and a line finally finished to the North Missouri Railroad at Coatesville.

Early in 1870, Gilman had boasted that the whole line from Marshalltown to Albia would be ready for iron by the first of August. That target date was not realized, however, and October still found "three gangs of track-layers at different points [who were] laying about two miles per day." Undaunted, the road announced that "iron and

other materials for the line from Marshalltown to Albia [were] on the ground, or on the way to it, and without some unforeseen accident, this portion of the road [would be] in running order in from 60 to 90 days and trains [would] then run through from St. Louis to St. Paul" via the Central route.[15]

As 1870 came to a close, Gilman had 105 miles of track in operation and the line was fully operational between Mason City and Marshalltown. At the same time, all grading had been completed on the route between Marshalltown and Albia. Winter did not halt construction; Gilman ordered rail-laying crews to start from Albia and Marshalltown, believing that two crews, working toward each other, could finish the project in half the time. Of course track would sink into the mud when "frost went out of the ground," but at least the line would be completed.

To some observers it appeared that Gilman was not sufficiently diligent in pushing the road south to the St. Louis connection. Not so. President Gilman did everything within his power to push the Central on to the Missouri border. Time was not on Gilman's side, however, and delay in reaching Coatesville proved costly. The North Missouri had given the "old" Iowa Central project as well as Gilman's road significant if uneven moral support over the years, but eventually its promoters and backers became frustrated by what they considered delay or lethargy. Up in the North Star State, M&StL's William D. Washburn took a very different position. "If St. Louis had one-tenth the energy and sagacity displayed by the Philadelphia, Baltimore, Chicago, Milwaukee, Iowa, and Minnesota men," he bellowed in 1871, "she would have had her iron horse bounding red-hot over our Minnesota frontier long ago." Indeed, said Washburn in disgust, "St. Louis is a slow coach in these days of railroad advancement." In any event, North Missouri withdrew its support, turning its affections to a CRCI competitor, the St. Louis & Cedar Rapids Railroad, with its line from

Coatesville to Bloomfield and Ottumwa. This road subsequently was leased to North Missouri, which operated the line as its "Iowa Extension." This defection was a bitter pill. Gilman might have finished the Albia–Coatesville extension anyway, but fate was to intervene, and the Central would have to wait for its long-desired St. Louis connections.[16]

Before the end of 1870, rails were in place for several miles north of Albia. On the opposite end of this construction zone, Grinnell was about to welcome its second railroad, as the Chicago, Rock Island & Pacific (CRI&P) had reached the Poweshiek County seat a few years earlier. Josiah B. Grinnell, the town's luminary, had been active in railroad affairs for a number of years and long had preached the value of a north-south road through central Iowa. To achieve this end, he had been elected president of a "paper road," the St. Louis, Iowa & St. Paul Railway, in 1858, and now he actively supported the Central by subscribing $5,000 in capital stock and $7,500 in construction stock. Thus he was an exceedingly proud man when he witnessed the entrance of CRCI into the community bearing his name. The *Poweshiek County Herald,* which proclaimed itself "independent in everything; neutral in nothing," described in detail the arrival of the Central's first train and the ensuing celebration:

> Preparations were made during the day to have a good time generally, when the last rail was laid down on the Central at the crossing of the C.R.I.&P. Railroad, at which time also, the first train from the North was expected with an excursion party from Eldora and Marshalltown.
>
> At three o'clock p.m. the last rail was laid down and spiked—the cannon boomed—the Stars and Stripes waved from the housetops, and the Hurrahs from the multitude were shouted in chorus with the first whistle on the Central at Grinnell!

After the speaking the excursionists were escorted to the cars where several barrels of sweet cider and apples invitingly greeted them—all partook of the good things presented. The party went aboard, the train moved off, and our citizens retired to their homes, satisfied with the day's proceedings—and content in knowing that the Central Railroad of Iowa was a success—and its completion to Grinnell a fixed fact.[17]

Track workers labored on, and soon rails were pushed northward to Mahaska County and Oskaloosa by the "Albia crew," while another group worked toward them. Mahaska residents had earlier contributed upward of $130,000 in local subscriptions to the "old" Iowa Central, and only now were they seeing the fruition of that sacrifice. The first of February saw the track gangs almost within sight of each other, and President Gilman ordered that a "last spike ceremony" be held at the North Skunk River bridge between Searsboro and New Sharon on February 4, 1871. Gilman sent telegrams to numerous businessmen and other notables along the line, inviting them to board special trains that would convey them to the place where the last spike was to be driven.[18]

Editor J. M. Chamberlain of the *Poweshiek County Herald* was among those who had been invited to view the completion of the Central's main line. Here is his description of the trip down from Grinnell:

> The day was bright and beautiful. A cannon was mounted upon a platform car, a telegrapher with all necessary furnishings was secured, and when the train rolled in from the north, the spacious platforms of the Union Depot were covered with citizens who had come to show their interest and secure a ride if accommodations would allow. But when the long and elegant train began to show its contents, as throngs piled out, this hope van-

ished. Visitors swarmed over the town filling hotels and restaurants and other sources of provisions.

After a delay of an hour, all were packed or repacked with the addition of about 75 from Grinnell, and all moved off to the firing of the cannon and waving of flags. A half hour brought us to Searsboro, the first station which has sprung up on the Central and named in honor of our worthy townsman. Three or four miles further and we were upon the classic Chicaqua—alias Skunk—where the great event was to take place.[19]

With a "special" and a "doubleheader" coal train standing on the south and a "special" and lumber train standing on the north. The last rail was [put] down and a polished spike, represented as that famous last spike of which we all have read and longed to see, was driven. At 5:15 o'clock Pres. Gilman took the sledge . . . and handed it to F. W. H. Sheffield, president of the construction company, who struck the spike a fine lick and surrendered the sledge to Judge Seevers who swung it around to the great risk of all bystanders, hit the rail a lively whack that would have done credit to any Irishman on the line, and then tried to play "shenanigan" and get another lick at it, but after several indifferent attempts to hit it, gave up to Gen. G. M. Woodbury. He was followed by Hon. J. B. Grinnell, who spotted it after a trial or two, and then Pres. Gilman took the hammer and drove home the spike to cheers, shouts, screeches, of 5 locomotives, music, etc. The spike was driven about 30 ft. this side of the county line [in Poweshiek County].[20]

With this joining of the last rails, the road was complete from Mason City to Albia. Charles Carroll Gilman was in large measure responsible

for this achievement, and now he had a few words to say to a very happy audience. Beginning his speech, Gilman pointed to the north and then to the south before saying: "Gentlemen, we have brought them together. To southern Iowa we have brought the lumber of Minnesota; to northern Iowa and Minnesota we introduce the cheap fuel, the magnificent coal of Mahaska county." The celebration concluded, business could get under way.[21]

Spring found the Central's rails down in the mud as forecast, but the company's management worked quickly to shore up the new line and to get ballast under its ties as quickly as possible. While there were frequent derailments, the road's promoters could be proud that it was open and operating over its entire length. The economy of the country was strong, and the company's bonds soon were sold. Grading operations were started on the stretch from Mason City to the Minnesota border, and track gangs would follow in due course.

Meanwhile, the Central's management was faced with the prospect of securing more motive power to move the burgeoning freight and passenger traffic. By now the road was operating numerous freight trains and work trains, and a daily passenger train was assigned in each direction over the entire line. The company had secured two locomotives from the Iowa River Railway, and now it purchased additional power. All were 4-4-0 American Standard engines with approximately the same specifications. The locomotive roster as of August 1871 is given in Table 5.1.

As summer changed to fall, rails were nearing Northwood, twenty miles north of Mason City, just short of the Minnesota–Iowa border. Meanwhile, the Central's management had to make a decision soon as to where it would locate permanent facilities for the shopping of its engines and cars. The Eldora Railroad & Coal Company had established elementary facilities at Eldora, and the Iowa River Railway had used and expanded them. The company later moved its corporate headquarters from

Table 5.1. Locomotive roster, August 1871

Engine number	Name	Manufacturer	Service	Division
1	*Thomas Kensett*	McKay & Aldus	Passenger	South
2	*H. P. Liscomb*	Hinckley	Freight	South
3	*Horace Abbott*	Hinckley	Freight	North
4	*W. B. Shattuck*	Hinckley	Freight	South
5	*John S. Gilman*	Hinckley	Passenger	North
6	*W. H. Seevers*	Hinckley	Passenger	South
7	*F. H. Sheffield*	Hinckley	Freight	South
8	*A. L. Hatch*	Hinckley	Freight	North
9	*R. A. Babage*	Hinckley	Freight	North
10	*J. M. Cate*	Manchester	Freight	South
11	*G. M. Woodbury*	Manchester	Freight	South
12	*C. C. Gilman*	Mason	Freight	North

Sources: Means, "Minneapolis & St. Louis Railroad," 43; Central Railroad Company of Iowa, *Locomotive Statement for the Month of August 1871*; Marshalltown Times-Republican, *June 6, 1949.*

Eldora to Marshalltown, and when one Henry Anson, a resident of that Marshall County community, donated nearly ten acres of land between Center Street and Third Avenue, Central officials decided to move all remaining facilities to Marshalltown. Work was started shortly thereafter on the various shop buildings, but not until 1875 were the shops fully moved from Eldora to Marshalltown.[22]

Residents of Worth County around Northwood were similarly generous toward the Central, giving it all the swamplands in the county (estimated at thirty-two thousand acres) in consideration for the company's grading, bridging, and culverting a line of road through the county. As a further incentive, Worth voters approved a tax that provided a $15,985.20 construction "donation." Prominent citizens also provided land for depot grounds, tracks, and yards valued at $2,000. Worth County clearly was hungry for a railroad, and that hunger was appeased when the first train steamed into Northwood on October 10, 1871. The grade north to the Minnesota border was finished the same season, but the rails ended just beyond the Northwood depot. Perhaps, thought local observers, the track

gangs were simply stopping for the winter; a push to the border seemed likely for the next year.[23]

The Central now had 185 miles of route in operation. The year-end statistics for 1871 showed operating revenues of $310,513.11 against operating expenses and taxes of $166,382.21. The future looked good. *Poor's Manual* for 1871 reported that the road owned 16 passenger cars, 5 mail cars, 300 coal cars, and 212 boxcars. During the final months of the year, CRCI added the motive power shown in Table 5.2.

Table 5.2. Added motive power, 1871

Engine number	Name	Builder
13	*Volunteer*	Manchester
14	*Advance*	Manchester
15	*P. V. Rogers*	Manchester
16	*J. C. Hoadley*	Manchester
17	*J. J. Donaldson*	Mason
18	*W. H. Wheelock*	Mason
19	*George Bliss*	Mason
20	*H. W. Eastman*	Mason

Source: Means, "Minneapolis & St. Louis Railroad Company," 43.

The year 1871 had been momentous. The road had been completed from southern Iowa nearly to the Minnesota border, and revenues from its operation were sufficient to pay the required interest on bonds. The year was to bow out with the national economy moving steadily upward, and there was no reason to suspect that things would be different in 1872. Surely, Gilman reasoned, the products of Iowa would be in demand, traffic would be good, the line would be fully completed, and the promoters would be happy.

The country's economy did, in fact, expand for most of 1872, and there was widespread prosperity and expansion within the railroad industry. In January the Central paid the interest due on its bonds, but as the year wore on it became evident that real prosperity had eluded the Iowa enterprise. The Central chose not to pursue its building plans on either end of the line. Consequently, the road, for all practical purposes, started nowhere and ended nowhere. Of course the line was open for traffic to the north in conjunction with the Milwaukee & St. Paul Railroad at Mason City, but that company curiously exhibited only modest interest in fostering business connections. On the other end of the line, there was still no real outlet to the south with the exception of the Burlington & Missouri River Railroad at Albia and the Des Moines Valley Company at Givin.[24]

During the late summer and early fall of 1872 there was a flurry of imagined activity around Northwood that implied the Central would soon be expanding into Albert Lea; one report had CRCI cars rolling over those rails before November 1. The *Minneapolis Tribune* even reported that the Central's trains would soon find themselves in the Mill City, taking a westward turn from Albert Lea over the Southern Minnesota Railroad, thence moving northward up that company's planned extension to Mankato, proceeding by means of a trackage agreement over St. Paul & Sioux City to Sioux City Junction, and finally driving into Minneapolis over M&StL. This was pure fiction, but the story acidly demonstrated the Central's dilemma and frustration over being stubbed at Northwood.[25]

On a brighter note, there was a marked increase in coal loadings and passenger traffic during 1872. Nevertheless, disappointing returns from the movement of grains and other commodities dimmed the picture. Undaunted, Gilman ordered expenditures for side tracks, waterworks, snow fences, depots, and machine shops and a roundhouse at Marshalltown. Furthermore, Gilman ordered four passenger cars, one hundred boxcars, and various other equipment aggregating $222,019 in expense.[26]

General freight agent J. W. Gilman released annual statistics showing the following volumes of grain loaded at the Central's stations, bound for the destinations indicated:

For St. Louis	1,528 cars
For Chicago	1,287 cars
For Milwaukee	829 cars
For St. Paul/Minneapolis	431 cars
For other points	1,218 cars

With the exception of St. Louis grain delivered to Des Moines Valley at Givin or to Burlington & Missouri River at Albia, much of the remaining grain traffic headed for Chicago or Milwaukee, short-hauling the Iowa road, because cars had to be handed to one of the Chicago trunk lines. The Central, of course, crossed all Chicago trunk roads in Iowa, and the local company obviously did not handle grain shipments for any great distance. A breakdown of remaining traffic saw coal clearly in the lead (4,971 cars), followed by cattle and hogs (1,093 cars), lumber (427 cars), and potatoes and onions (398 cars). A total of 17,398 cars were billed in 1872, with the top ten stations ranked as follows:

1. Oskaloosa—5,661 cars
2. Marshalltown—1,457 cars
3. Eldora—750 cars
4. Union—651 cars
5. New Sharon—625 cars
6. Steamboat Rock—616 cars
7. Ackley—614 cars

Figure 5.2. Oskaloosa, from which this "maid of all work" is about to depart, was Central's most important billing point.

8. Liscomb—538 cars
9. Albion—504 cars
10. Mason City—485 cars[27]

Moreover, CRCI's general passenger agent announced that a total of 87,941 passengers had been carried in 1872. At an average rate of 4.64 cents per mile, this service generated $133,132.07 in revenue for the year. Local ticket sales accounted for the bulk of these receipts. During the last week of March 1872, the agent at Searsboro sold thirty-two full fares (twenty-three of them to nearby Grinnell) and four half-fares (children under 12); that volume was likely typical for similar-sized stations up and down the line. The Central also did a good inter-line business at all junctions, with the Burlington & Missouri River connection at Albia accounting for the largest number of such passengers in 1872.[28]

In 1872, President Gilman's road had earned

$440,829.26 in freight revenues, $133,122.07 in passenger revenues, and $40,109.68 in revenues for express, mail, and other services. The total was $614.071.01 against operating expenses of $432,160.06. The road had shown a profit from operations, but its surplus, sad to say, was not sufficient to meet the interest on its bonds, payment of which it had defaulted on July 15.[29]

Gilman's great expectations were coming to naught, and there was no prospect of recovery for a road that could not pay its interest even in good times. Gilman faced a bleak future as 1872 drew to a close. His road was completed in neither direction, bond interest was unpaid, repairs and ordinary expenditures were held so low that the railroad was becoming a dangerous property, and a competitor was building north from Burlington through Cedar Rapids to some northern point in the Central's trade area.[30]

CENTRAL RAIL ROAD OF IOWA.

Weekly Local Ticket Report.

From *Searsboro* Station, for Week ending *April* 1872

DESTINATION.	Commencing Number.	Closing Number.	No. Sold.	RATE.	AMOUNT.	No. Sold.	RATE.	AMOUNT.	No. Sold.	RATE.	AMOUNT.
			WHOLE TICKETS.			HALF TICKETS.			EXCURSION TICKETS.		
Northwood	0										
Mason City,	2										
Linn Grove,	0							2.75				
Chapin,	0							8.25				
Hampton,	2											
Faulkner,	0											
Ackley,	6											
Abbott,	0											
Steamboat Rock,	0											
Eldora,	1											
Union,	9											
Liscomb,	6											
Albion,	18											
Marshalltown,	57	61	1.85	4	7.40							
Gilman,	21	24	1.10	3	3.30							
Grinnell,	652	667	55	15	8.25	1	30	30			
Searsboro,												
New Sharon,	192	193	45	1	45						
Oskaloosa,	293	296	1.05	3	3.15						
Eddyville,	32										
Coal Field	0										
Albia,	64										
Genera	0										
Half Tickets,	90	91	1								
Excursion Tickets	105										

Figure 5.3. The agent at Searsboro turned in an encouraging report of ticket sales for the last week of March 1872.

Chapter 6
THE TANGLED WAYS OF FINANCE

*Thereupon Judge Dillon declined to make any order or sanction, outside the
narrow range of . . . [Receiver Grinnell's] service. This by the opinion of owners and
sagacious Iowa men, depreciated the property millions of dollars and invited what occurred—
an occupancy of the territory by rival companies. The Central was doomed
to be only a local road without any power of self-assertion.*
—JOSIAH BUSHNELL GRINNELL, *MEN AND EVENTS OF FORTY YEARS*

PRESIDENT GILMAN AND HIS IOWA BACKERS
long since had been forced to yield financial
control of the Central Railroad Company
of Iowa in order to gain capital sufficient to
see the road built. It augured ill for them;
when the company defaulted on its second
mortgage interest on April 15, 1873, Eastern
bankers and investors, who held a majority
of the bonds, decided that there should be a change
in management.[1]

Charles Gilman and his administration left in
bitterness. Theirs had been the energy that had
given the road its impetus, and now they were
thrust out of office under fire and without thanks.
Gilman himself would fight the new management
for a number of years. Meanwhile, the energetic
native of Maine invested in coal mining operations
near Oskaloosa; his efforts resulted in the establish-
ment of Consolidated Coal Company, of which he
was president. The Central was called upon to build
a spur from its main line south of Oskaloosa to the
tipple near Muchakinock. This mining operation
met with extraordinary success under Gilman's
direction, and the Central enjoyed lucrative traffic
on its Muchakinock Spur.[2]

The Central's new management team
consisted of Isaac M. Cate as president and
D. N. Pickering as superintendent; it was
given a cool reception by both long-time
employees and minority stock- and bondholders. Under the Cate administration,
there was another attempt to consolidate
operations at Marshalltown, but this was
not entirely accomplished until 1875, and the new
president was no more successful than his predecessor in getting the line built to completion on
either end. Local passenger traffic and coal business
increased in spite of the secondary postwar depression that had started in 1873, but shipments of other
commodities showed no gain, and the road still
failed to pay the interest due on its bonds.

Not surprisingly, then, major bondholders
again looked for solutions to their problems. Even
before the demise of the Gilman regime, efforts
had been made to join the Central with the fledgling Minneapolis & St. Louis Railroad, which had
aspirations of linking the two cities of its corporate
name. In 1871 M&StL had built a line of road from
Minneapolis to a junction with the St. Paul & Sioux
City Railroad near Carver, Minnesota, and by the

40

end of 1871, the Central had been opened from Northwood to Albia.

H. T. Welles, the first president of M&StL, spent six weeks of the winter of 1872–73 in New York for the purpose of effecting a consolidation of the Minneapolis & St. Louis and the Central Railroad of Iowa with the Northern Pacific, which would give the latter a potential connection with St. Louis. Welles was unsuccessful, and with the failure of Jay Cooke & Company on September 18, 1873, all hope of attachment to the Northern Pacific vanished. Another suitor had to be found if the road was to be sold or leased.[3]

At the same time, the Central was faced with severe competition from the Burlington, Cedar Rapids & Minnesota Railroad (BCR&M), which had completed a line of road from Burlington to a point near the Central in northern Iowa, passing through Cedar Rapids, Waterloo, Cedar Falls, and Nora Springs to rest at a remote location labeled Plymouth Junction. BCR&M had a good southern connection at Burlington and served burgeoning communities, but yet, like the Central, it was "stuck" at a northern outpost. It did have trackage rights over Milwaukee & St. Paul from Plymouth Junction to Austin, where it formed its northern terminal, but this was not at all satisfactory for the Cedar Rapids company. Nevertheless, also like the Central, BCR&M was short of funds, and these arrangements, its management concluded, would have to suffice for the time being.[4]

For the Central, the year 1874 was much like the one just past—except that the road's problems were even more acute. Adding to its operating expense for the year was a bill of $16,280 that the road paid for "shoveling snow." Even the weather, Cate must have concluded, was conspiring against the Iowa company. The national economy continued its downward trend, and bondholders, a number of whom had been partially or totally wiped out by the panic of 1873, were almost frantic in their desire either to obtain the interest due them or to dump their securities. But it was hard to sell securities in 1874, and harder still to make the Central earn enough to pay the interest due.[5]

A group of bondholders who called themselves the New York Committee controlled the road at the time, but a dissident group styled the Boston Committee owned or controlled a large minority of the company. These two groups were at odds over corporate policy, and the infighting soon reached monumental proportions, with both sides issuing volumes of printed propaganda. Action started on February 19, 1874, when H. J. Boardman, Charles Alexander, and A. V. Lynch were appointed to represent the Boston group as a "Committee of Three." They quickly acted to institute a suit in the U.S. Circuit Court, District of Iowa, in the name of Charles Alexander et al., seeking that the desired relief be decreed and that, in the interim, a disinterested, capable man be appointed by the court to act as receiver. Subsequently the trustee, Farmers Loan & Trust Company, consented to "move in the matter" and was substituted as plaintiff instead of Alexander et al.[6]

The object of the Boston group was to force foreclosure and sale of the property "in order that its possession and control might pass into the hands of those entitled to it under the mortgage"—in other words, the bondholders. The Boston group, numbering Gilman and most of the Iowa holders, hoped to sell the property or lease it to a strong western road, and with this in mind made overtures to the redoubtable Russell Sage, whom some had labeled "Old Ready Cash" and who had withstood all onslaughts during the "Ten Days of Terror" that had marked the panic of 1873. The wily Sage just might be able to rescue the Iowa bondholders by purchasing or leasing the Central. At least that was the hope of the Boston Committee.[7]

Meanwhile, New York bondholders held a meeting on July 31 in the railroad company's New

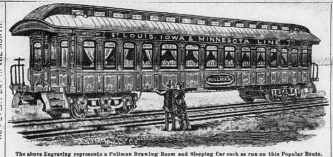
Figure 6.1. Wabash predecessor St. Louis, Kansas City & Northern took the lead in advertising St. Louis–St. Paul service via the Central. New York and Boston bondholders found nothing to quarrel about when that road boosted Central's traffic.

York office. This assembly elected a "Committee of Six" to act on behalf of the New York first and second mortgage bondholders. The Committee of Six resisted efforts of the Boston bondholders, inspected the property, and submitted a summary of their work to the New York group on November 24. According to the committee, the Central's current management was operating the road "faithfully and honestly . . . with probably as reasonable success as could be expected, in view of the many embarrassing circumstances with which the management is surrounded." President Cate had inherited from the Gilman administration an estimated debt of $100,000 in unpaid wages, not to mention various notes on rolling stock that were past due. In the end, the Committee of Six recommended to the New York bondholders' group that all debts be paid and that rails be extended from Northwood to the state line. Finally, the committee suggested that, if and when the road got back on its financial feet, the interest due on the bonds be paid to the respective owners.[8]

At about the same time, Superintendent D. N. Pickering was appointed "provisional receiver" of the property; the road was now under the direct supervision of the court, an arrangement favored by both the Boston and the New York committees.

The major issue separating the two groups was disposition of the road. The Boston membership wanted sale or lease of the property to another company, but the New York group favored a program designed to restore the road—provided the Iowa company could be reinvigorated without great hardship to the bondholders. The latter group did not feel, as the Boston Committee proposed, that the Central was so strategically located that *any* rival concern would gladly assume the property by lease or sale. The New Yorkers also pointed out that the Iowa line bisected a sizable number of east-west trunk lines, and if any one of these were to lease the north-south Central, all other connecting carriers would immediately cancel favorable interchange

agreements with the Iowa company; a loss of revenue would be the obvious result of this policy, and the value of Central bonds would be decreased accordingly. The New York Committee simply concluded that their investment was more secure if bondholders retained possession of the Central Railroad Company of Iowa.[9]

The Boston Committee responded by pointing out that they had contacted Russell Sage, who had indicated that Milwaukee & St. Paul would offer "an out and out proposition for an alliance." In advocating lease of the Iowa company to Milwaukee & St. Paul, the Boston Committee observed that all major trunk lines in the Hawkeye State were currently leased "to larger corporations on a percentage of gross earnings of 28 to 35 per cent."[10]

On December 26, 1874, the Boston Committee proposed formation of a company styled the St. Louis, Iowa & Minnesota Railroad. It further proposed that this new firm purchase the "Central Railroad of Iowa, with all its property, franchises, privileges and power to construct and complete" the line from Albia to the Missouri border and from Northwood to the Minnesota boundary. This transaction was to involve an exchange of securities, with the new road expected to pick up all previous debt. The main goal of the Bostonians was to secure control of the Central and then to lease or sell the property, but to facilitate lease or sale of the company, they thought, it would be necessary to extend the line to the Missouri and Minnesota borders.[11]

The Farmers Loan & Trust Company, acting as trustee, was neutral in the struggle for control. As new proposals were offered by the respective committees, however, the bank was obligated to forward such information and solicit subsequent bondholder sentiment. Therefore, in response to the Boston Committee's proposal to establish the St. Louis, Iowa & Minnesota Railroad, on December 30, 1874, Farmers Loan & Trust sent bondholders' petitions to all those holding Central

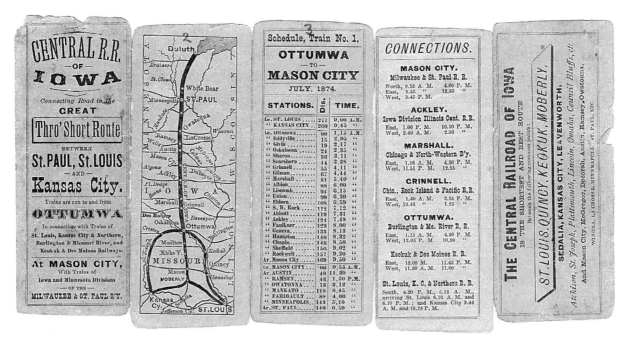

Figure 6.2. In 1874, the Central issued tiny accordion-style timetables especially targeting business travelers.

Railroad Company of Iowa bonds. It was up to these security holders to decide if they favored the plan.[12]

Before results of the Boston Committee's proposal could be learned, a compromise was drawn up. This offered an additional alternative in the form of yet another proposed company—reorganization of the Central Railroad Company of Iowa into the Central Iowa Railway. Boardman, Alexander, and Lynde—all members of the Boston Committee, which had filed the earlier suit of foreclosure—were members of the new "joint" committee, which also included leading figures of the New York group. Richard L. Ashurst, representing the bankrupt estate of Jay Cooke & Company, was joined by Thomas Reed and John H. B. Latrobe, among others, who found themselves working closely with their former rivals from the Boston group.[13]

The proposed Central Iowa Railway would be designed to acquire the Central Railroad Company of Iowa through an exchange of securities favoring various classes of bondholders of the older company. Interest on bonds falling due January 15,

1876—and thereafter for a period of five years, or until January 15, 1881—would be forgiven so that the new road could finally finish building the line to the northern and southern borders of Iowa. In lieu of interest payments on the bonds, holders were to be issued preferred stock, while creditors and common stockholders were to receive new common stock. Between the time that the road was to emerge from the hands of the receiver and the date of the first annual election (proposed for 1882), the road was to be governed by a joint executive committee that, for that period of time, would have the power to operate the road or lease it to another carrier if necessary.[11]

By October 1875, a judgment had been rendered in favor of the joint committee; the court ordered a decree of foreclosure. But before action could be taken to put the Central into the hands of the joint committee, minority bondholders representing a mere $200,000 of the total bonds outstanding appealed the decision to the Supreme Court of Iowa. The effect of this appeal would be to tie up the property for some time. The railroad remained in the hands of D. N. Pickering, superintendent and receiver, until January 14, 1876, when, in a surprising development, the court appointed Josiah Bushnell Grinnell receiver of the road. The court, under Judge John F. Dillon, felt no prejudice toward receiver Pickering, but indicated that the jobs of superintendent and receiver should be vested in two separate persons.[15]

Grinnell long had been interested in the development of Iowa railroads, donating much time and money to the construction of a number of companies. He had invested in CRCI and had served on its board. He was, however, by no means a major shareholder; the court apparently felt that he would have no intense pecuniary interest in the company. Grinnell had been advised by many associates not to accept the challenge of renovating the road, but he summarily rejected that advice.

Isaac Cate, president of the road since Gilman's departure, was immediately critical of Grinnell. The initial problem concerned Pickering, whom Grinnell retained on the job during the first part of 1876. Pickering incurred the displeasure of the receiver, however, when he criticized the latter's plan to cut and sell ice, readily available in Iowa during the winter, to consumers in the St. Louis area. At any rate, Pickering was asked to leave the road, and he soon made his way to the protective custody of a much-incensed Isaac Cate and the joint committee in New York. The dismissal of Pickering surprised nobody on the local scene, but brought an instantaneous complaint from New York. Pickering, while becoming less and less favored by his employees and customers served by the Central, had become the joint committee's fair-haired boy in 1875 when, under his tutelage, the Central posted freight and passenger earnings that combined to produce the highest total revenue in the company's history. The road's operating expenses, maintenance, and capital expenditures had been held to minimal standards, but gross income figures were of a nature that could be easily understood by the joint committee.

Figure 6.3. Idealistic Josiah Bushnell Grinnell was appointed receiver early in 1876.

Therefore, they saw little to be happy about in the dismissal of Pickering.[16]

Grinnell immediately sought to implement some of his own economies. He used money from the sale of ice to pacify restless employees who had become increasingly and understandably disgruntled because they were paid irregularly—if at all. Next Grinnell ordered the number of non-operating employees cut to the bone. He followed this move by issuing a decree "limiting Sunday service to an absolute necessity" and ending the practice of making extra compensation available to those whom necessity forced to work on the Sabbath.[17]

Grinnell was possessed of a stern paternalistic bent. When he found the deportment of company employees to be less than what he considered respectable, he posted the following edict: "Any person in the train service carrying intoxicating drinks stealthily for others, or any employee using the same, will be dismissed for this offense; also for the use of profane or ungentlemanly language to the patrons of the railroad." Apparently the habits of the employees improved under the careful guidance of Grinnell, for some months later he observed that "the morals of the employees—numbering six hundred—had been improved."[18]

Grinnell found no devices to facilitate needed construction on either end of the railroad, but he did cozy up to Russell Sage, asking for advice on the building of certain branch lines designed to feed the Central's main trunk. Sage "agreed to furnish money and take receiver's certificates" sufficient to build one branch to the "What Cheer coal mines" and another feeder to Grundy Center if the Central chose to move in those directions. Eventually Sage also agreed to put up money sufficient to extend the road to some St. Paul connection, but Judge Dillon chose not to approve any of these measures.[19]

Grinnell incurred further criticism from various bondholders when he began to upgrade the property. Upon inspection he found a sizable hole in the roof of the new machine shop at Marshalltown and, by inquiry, learned that when it rained all work in the shop ceased. He ordered the hole patched and then proceeded to set up reforms designed to see that wood milled in the shops was sawed and planed by steam power instead of by hand, as had been the procedure theretofore. Locomotive wheels had been shipped over one hundred miles to be "turned" by a competitor, but now Grinnell bought equipment to allow the work to be done at Marshalltown. The danger of a disastrous roundhouse fire was acute (and there already had been one such conflagration) because oil was stored in unsafe locations. This, too, was corrected. Track scales were absent on the road, and the receiver immediately ordered them. Moreover, side tracks were extended and yard facilities enlarged at various terminals.

The idealistic Josiah Grinnell moved from station to station ordering reforms into effect. Newspapers of the area long had advised travelers to guard their lives by avoiding travel on the Central, and jokes about the road's poor performance had become legend. Accounts of the comings and goings of one Eli Perkins mixed fact, fiction, and humor, but accurately reflected public perception of the level of the Central's service at the time. Perkins, it seems, gave a lecture at Osage one winter evening and then traveled by sleigh to Mason City, where he tottered to the door of the Central's depot and asked the agent if the "five o'clock train" had left for Grinnell, where he was expected that evening for another presentation. The agent, Perkins related, gave him an incredulous look. "Gone, man! Why she went last September," exclaimed the agent. "She is a summer train. But . . . she will go again in June. If you must go on her you can sit around here in the depot and wait." But Perkins was adamant that he had to be in Grinnell that evening for an important lecture and demanded that the agent wire the Central's President J. B. Grinnell. As the story goes, when Grinnell heard of Perkins's dilemma, he ordered out an engine and crew to whisk this important personage to his appointment in the seat of Poweshiek County. It must have been a memorable trip. "Oh, how we did fly," reported Perkins. "Hampton looked like one long house. . . . Villages became splotches of maroon paint. Telegraph poles blurred like wagon spokes in the sun." The engineer blew the whistle, "but the train beat the sound into Marshalltown, and the agent came out [and] looked the wrong way. We had passed the town, and the whistle was still behind. In fact, we were five miles beyond Gilman when the whistle came loafing into that place." Perkins arrived in time to deliver his lecture, but when he attempted to relate the story of his marvelous trip on the Central the audience hooted him down; Perkins lost his "reputation for veracity" among those who knew that

TIME SCHEDULE

THROUGH BETWEEN

St. Paul and Minneapolis, St. Louis and Kansas City,

—)VIA THE(—

CHICAGO, MILWAUKEE & ST. PAUL, CENTRAL OF IOWA, AND ST. LOUIS, KANSAS CITY & NORTHERN RAILWAYS.

In Effect June, 1878.

ROADS OF LINE.	GOING NORTH. Distance from St. Louis.	GOING NORTH. ST. PAUL EXPRESS. No. 3. Daily.	GOING NORTH. MINNEAPOLIS EXPRESS. No. 1. Daily except Sunday.	STATIONS Between Terminal Points of the Line.	GOING SOUTH. KANSAS CITY EXPRESS. No. 2. Daily except Sunday.	GOING SOUTH. ST. LOUIS EXPRESS. No. 4. Daily.	GOING SOUTH. Distance from St. Paul.	ROADS OF LINE.
C, M. & St. P. Ry.	588	6.50 A.M.	6.27 P.M.	Ar. ST. PAUL Le.	6.10 A.M.	8.25 P.M.	0	C, M. & St. P. Ry
	591	6.55	6.43	Minneapolis	6.00	8.20	0	
	582	6.25	6.05	St. Paul Junction	6.40	9.05	6	
	578	6.22	6.02	Bluff Side Track	6.44	9.10	8	
	573	6.02	5.50	Westcott	6.57	9.30	13	
	568	5.38	5.30	Rosemount	7.12	9.54	19	
	561	5.10	5.10	Farmington	7.82	10.22	26	
	554	4.42	4.51	Castle Rock	7.55	10.50	33	
	548	4.18	4.34	Northfield	8.10	11.14	39	
	545	4.06	4.25	Dundas	8.19	11.26	42	
	538	3.38	4.04	Erin	8.38	11.54	49	
	534	3.23	3.51	Faribault	8.50	12.10 A.M.	53	
	530	3.06	3.41	Wolcott	8.59	12.26	57	
	525	2.46	3.27	Medford	9.13	12.46	62	
	519	2.22	3.10	Owatonna	9.30	1.10	68	
	514	1.58	2.54	Somersett	9.45	1.34	73	
	510	1.46	2.44	Aurora	9.54	1.46	77	
	501	1.03	2.18	Blooming Prairie	10.15	2.22	86	
	492	12.26	1.54	Lansing	10.37	2.58	95	
	489	12.14	1.45	Ramsey	10.45	3.10	98	
	486	12.02 A.M.	d 1.35 P.M.	Austin	d11.35	3.30	101	
	475	11.00 P.M.	10.43 A.M.	Lyle	12.05 P.M.	4.15	112	
	468	10.30	10.25	Carpenter	12.30	4.40	119	
	455	9.35	9.48	Plymouth	1.05	5.30	132	
	447	9.30 P.M.	9.30 A.M.	Le. Mason City Ar.	1.30 P.M.	6.00 A.M.	141	
C. R. R. of I.	447	9.30 P.M.	9.30 A.M.	Ar. Mason City Le.	1.30 P.M.	6.10 A.M.	141	C. R. R. of I.
	437	8.55	8.46	Rockwell	2.13	6.50	152	
	430	8.36	b 8.25	Sheffield	2.30	b 7.30	159	
	426	8.23	7.45	Chapin	2.42	7.45	162	
	420	8.03	7.24	Hampton	3.00	8.04	169	
	413	7.43	7.03	Geneva	3.16	8.23	175	
	408	7.27	6.46	Faulkner	3.29	8.37	180	
	404	7.13	6.32	Ackley	3.42	8.53	185	
	399	6.55	6.14	Abbott	3.55	9.08	190	
	392	6.34	5.51	Steamboat Rock	4.14	9.29	197	
	388	6.20	5.37	Eldora	4.25	9.43	200	
	382	6.03	5.17	Gifford	4.42	10.01	207	
	378	5.52	5.02	Union	4.52	10.12	210	
	373	5.37	4.49	Liscomb	5.06	10.27	215	
	368	5.20	4.30	Albion	5.20	10.43	221	
	360	s 4.55	4.05	Marshalltown	s 5.40	11.10	228	
	353	4.14	3.32	Dillon	6.20	11.31	235	
	346	3.55	3.08	Gilman	6.40	11.52	242	
	335	3.25	2.30	Grinnell	7.12	d12.25 P.M.	253	
	332	3.07	2.20	G. & M. Junction	7.21	1.06	257	
	324	2.40	1.56	Searsboro	7.45	1.33	265	
	315	2.10	1.30	New Sharon	8.10	2.10	273	
	308	1.27	12.50	Oskaloosa	8.50	2.53	285	
	298	12.50 P.M.	12.15 A.M.	Eddyville	9.25	3.30	294	
	277	11.55 A.M.	11.20 P.M.	Le. Ottumwa Ar.	10.15 P.M.	4.20 P.M.	311	
St. L. K. C. & N. Ry.	277	11.30 A.M.	10.10 P.M.	Ar. Ottumwa Le.	10.15 P.M.	4.50 P.M.	311	St. L. K. C. & N. Ry.
	261	10.37	9.13	Belknap	10.59	5.45	327	
	256	10.20	8.57	Bloomfield	11.15	6.05	332	
	242	9.33	8 18	Moulton	11.50	6.52	343	
	227	8.45	7.43	Glenwood	12.25 A.M.	7.40	358	
	218	b 8.15	7.15	Queen City	12.48	s 8.30	367	
	203	7.08	6.35	Kirkville	1.27	9.20	382	
	160	5.27	s 5.05	Macon	2.55	11.10	416	
	146	4.20	3.45	Moberly	11.15	12.40 A.M.	442	
	132	3.07	2.43	Centralia	12.15 P.M.	1.36	468	
	108	2.35	2.09	Mexico	12.50	2.25	480	
	82	1.20	12.50	Montgomery	2.15	3.30	506	
	73	12.55	12.05 P.M.	High Hill	2.40	3.54	515	
	68	12.15 A.M.	11.27 A.M.	Warrenton	3.20	4.30	530	
	43	11.38 P.M.	10.47	Wentzville	4.00	5.04	545	
	21	10.41	9.54	St. Charles	4.54	5.52	567	
	10	10.05	9.15	Ferguson	5.30	6.25	578	
	0	9.20 P.M.	8.30 A.M.	Le. ST. LOUIS Ar.	6.15 P.M.	7.10 A.M.	588	
St. L.	129	12.30 A.M.	11.10 A.M.	Ar. Moberly Le.	4.10 A.M.	4.10 A.M.	442	St. L.
	108	11.30 P.M.	10.18	Salisbury	5.02	5.02	463	
	90	10.45	9.35	Brunswick	5.45	5.45	481	
	79	10.12	9.00	Miami	6.15	6.15	492	
	41	8.30	7.18	Lexington Junction	b 8.10	b 8.10	530	
	2	6.20	5.15	Harlem	9.57	9.57	569	
	0	6.05 P.M.	5.00 A.M.	Le. KANSAS CITY Ar.	10.12 A.M.	10.12 A.M.	571	

B—Breakfast.   D—Dinner.   S—Supper.

Pullman's Finest Drawing Room Sleeping Cars run through Daily on 3 and 4.

Leaving time of Nos. 1 and 3 at Mason City is Chicago time.   North of Mason City is St. Paul time.

Figure 6.4. Business picked up as the panic of 1873 eased, and more persons could be found aboard the elegant Pullman cars assigned to trains 3 and 4.

the road's track and motive power were inadequate to such a splendid performance. Indeed, according to Perkins, President Grinnell himself said privately that the Central "was not a railroad, but simply a branch line of the State Penitentiary at Fort Madison and that all convicts sent there over Central Railroad Company of Iowa were immediately released because Courts had ruled that it is unconstitutional to punish a man twice for the same offense."[20]

Josiah B. Grinnell may have quietly or mildly mocked the property for which he was responsible, but he continued—now with a missionary zeal—to straighten up the road by spending lots of money. It was a policy that pleased the road's customers, if not its bondholders. On he moved, replacing iron rail with steel, installing new ties, establishing new stations, ballasting the road with gravel purchased from on-line pits, widening cuts, putting up right-of-way and snow fences, paying taxes—and paying salaries.[21]

For 1876, the Central's operating receipts were down slightly from the year before, but its operating expenses were up sharply. Grinnell and Judge John F. Dillon received bouquets from most Iowans, but they received sharp and continuous rebuke from the East. Grinnell was especially harassed by backers of D. N. Pickering, while Judge Dillon was bombarded by complaints charging Grinnell with excessive expenditures and waste. Accusers also argued that Judge Dillon was secretly arranging to have a close relative buy the road once the current bondholders became completely disenchanted with the company and the operations of the current receiver. Both Grinnell and Dillon were eventually cleared of all charges, but neither man was to enjoy the prestige that had been his before these irresponsible accusations.[22]

After almost three years of work, anguish, and harassment, Grinnell resigned his post as receiver. The road's debts had been paid, its increased operating costs had been met, and Grinnell managed to turn over $53,000 in surplus to his successor. When Grinnell had taken office, first mortgage bonds were selling on the market for 32 cents on the dollar, but during his tenure these securities vacillated, surpassing par on one occasion. Grinnell received a commendation from the bench, and even his enemies must have agreed that the road was in better physical shape than when the property had been handed over to him.[23]

In an effort to completely vindicate his handling of the Central's affairs, Grinnell filed suit against parties who had harassed him. He was subsequently exonerated of all charges and even granted double compensation for his services. This verdict was appealed to the U.S. Supreme Court, but here again Grinnell was vindicated. So ended the Grinnell years.[24]

H. L. Morrill, "a railroad man of wide experience," became receiver of the Central Railroad Company of Iowa early in 1879. Morrill came to a renovated road that had seen the most profitable year of its history. The Railroad Commissioners of Iowa verified that the Central had made $841,835.35 in 1878 (up almost $100,000 over 1877) against operating expenses and taxes totaling $569,618.65 (up only $11,000 over 1877).[25]

All looked well for the Central, or so it seemed. Regrettably, though, more strong competitors had thrust their tentacles well into the service area of the Iowa company. A branch of the Chicago, Rock Island & Pacific had reached Oskaloosa in 1875, and a share of the heavy traffic that had once gone exclusively via the Central now left Mahaska County over rails of the "Great Rock Island Route." CRCI still claimed the lion's share of business from Oskaloosa, but on the far north end of the line things looked different.

In May 1877, Burlington, Cedar Rapids & Minnesota (reorganized as Burlington, Cedar Rapids & Northern, or BCR&N, on June 22, 1876) began construction of a short extension designed to connect Plymouth Junction with CRCI. Indeed, BCR&N

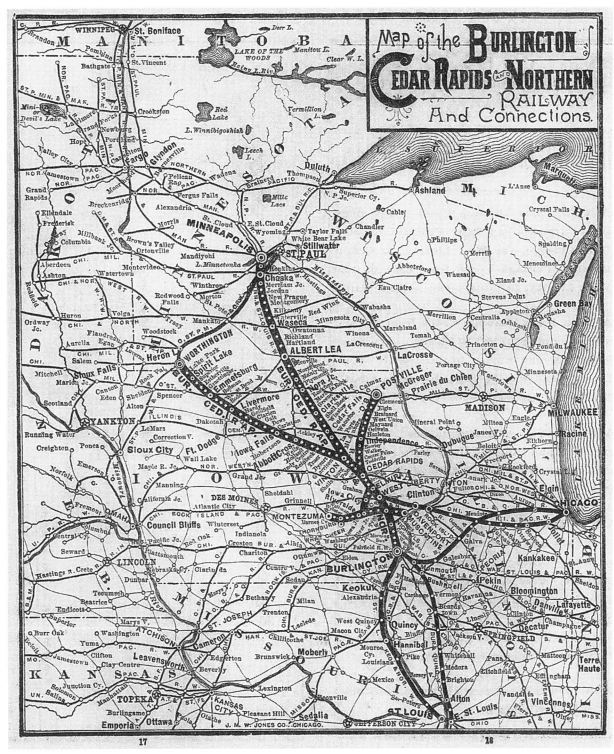

Map 6.1. Burlington, Cedar Rapids & Northern proved to be a strong contender, effectively preempting a desired Central connection with Minneapolis & St. Louis.

reached the Central at a point called Manly Junction, nine miles north of Mason City, and subsequently received trackage rights from the latter company to operate its trains to Northwood.[26]

Northwood residents had desperately wanted the Central to build to their community, and eventually the road had, of course, been built. Soon, though, the community tired of being "a one railroad town," and presently it had offered pecuniary inducements to the Cedar Rapids firm if it would build a line from Plymouth Junction to Northwood. BCR&N agreed to build west to the Central—provided that road would allow Cedar Rapids trains to operate into Northwood as competition. This was agreed to, BCR&N received a monetary bonus from Northwood, and Worth County anticipated the arrival of its second railroad. Accordingly, "at three o'clock on Wednesday afternoon, August 1, 1877, the first regular train of that company [BCR&N] steamed into Northwood with bell and whistle sounding." Now Northwood had two railroads, each coming in from the south on the same rails and each with the community of Northwood as its northernmost terminal—but not for long.[27]

Minneapolis & St. Louis had been pushing south from its junction with the St. Paul & Sioux City Railroad near Carver, Minnesota, and by this time it was headed for its Albert Lea objective. As soon as the Cedar Rapids road received trackage rights from Manly Junction to Northwood, its management consummated a traffic and terminal agreement with M&StL. BCR&N then set itself to the task of closing the short gap between Northwood and the Iowa–Minnesota state line with rails of its own. Ignoring the already located Central grade (from Northwood to the state line), BCR&N threw up another grade and laid track from a connection with Central rails north of the Northwood depot to a point just over the Minnesota border then called Shell Rock. The line from Northwood to Shell Rock was opened on August 15, 1877; M&StL owned the rails from Albert Lea down to the state boundary at Shell Rock and leased the same to the Cedar Rapids road. On November 11, 1879, M&StL reached Albert Lea from the north, and it was with considerable pleasure that M&StL and BCR&N announced that through Minneapolis–St. Louis freight and passenger service had been established via the Albert Lea gateway. And it was with sorrow that the Central Railroad Company of Iowa admitted it had been beaten out of a fine through connection of its own.[28]

Chapter 7
THE HOOK & EYE

I came here broke
And it was do or die,
So I hired out
On the Hook and Eye.
—POPULAR RHYME AMONG TRANSIENT EMPLOYEES

THE CENTRAL RAILROAD COMPANY OF IOWA had made a remarkable physical recovery under receiver Josiah Bushnell Grinnell. On July 18, 1877, Lewis M. Fisher, special master, requested that a master's deed to the property be given Farmers Loan & Trust Company of New York. This request was granted by the U.S. Circuit Court in Iowa, but the road remained in the hands of a receiver until it was reorganized as the Central Iowa Railway. On May 28, 1879, Farmers Loan & Trust agreed to deed the property to the new company, which was fully reorganized on June 4 and then announced that its officers were Isaac M. Cate, president; Russell Sage, vice president; D. N. Pickering, superintendent; Charles Alexander, secretary; and G. E. Taintor, assistant secretary.[1]

The capital of the new company was set at $7,000,000. First and second preferred stock was issued to holders of first and second bonds in order to fund the past-due interest on Central Railroad of Iowa bonds. Common stock was issued to former common stockholders and to creditors of the old company. The plan of finance was remarkably similar to what had been proposed by the "joint committee."[2]

Russell Sage long had been, as it were, "standing in the wings." Now, however, he assumed the vice presidency and was in a position to wield even more influence. Sage had been familiar with the Central for years, and in 1870 had built the branch to connect Milwaukee & St. Paul with the Iowa company at Mason City, giving the Central its northern outlet. Later he had offered the Boston Committee moral support in its struggles, and J. B. Grinnell, then receiver, had sought his advice and capital for proposed branch lines.

If independent routes to St. Louis and Minneapolis were closed to the Central, Sage pointed out, it would have to become a strong local road. To become such, he reasoned, the company needed feeders to contribute traffic for the main line. Accordingly President Cate was instructed to move quickly to secure local aid, buy property, and secure equipment for a number of potential routes.

As the new management issued orders for these surveys, it simultaneously reviewed the road's current strategic location. The avowed goal of all earlier managements had been to complete the road to connections on both its northern and its southern extremities. Without exception, every effort had failed. Recently the rival Burlington,

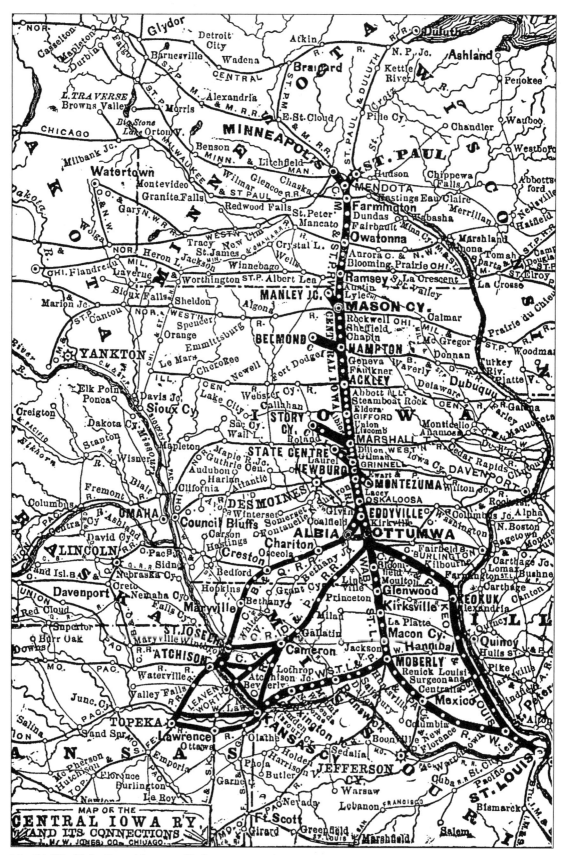

Map 7.1. Would the Central forever suffer from a truncated route structure? Map circa 1881.

Figure 7.1. The Central would have to become a strong local road, but that was a difficult assignment. Chicago roads laced the Central's service area with main arteries and an array of feeders such as that of Chicago & North Western at Gifford. The Central main line is in the foreground, its line to a company-owned gravel pit in the distance at upper left.

Cedar Rapids & Northern had, moreover, sealed off the hoped-for Minneapolis & St. Louis connection on the north. To the south, another attempt was made to construct the line from Albia to Moulton, about twenty-seven miles; a run had been made at St. Louis investors in 1873 seeking subscriptions for this project, but again without success. For that matter, the grade from Albia to Moulton and on to the Missouri state line, which had been purchased from the "old" Iowa Central by the Central Railroad Company of Iowa in 1869, had been lost to a competing railroad in a dramatic court fight. This latter development had proved a particularly ugly turn of events—the negative effect of which was compounded by the fact that yet another competitor was actively buying up land for a twenty-five-mile route south from Albia to Centerville. All independent avenues in that direction seemingly were

preempted, and it appeared that the Central would forever have to settle for Albia as its southernmost terminal.[3]

Back in 1875, before J. B. Grinnell had become receiver, he had organized the Grinnell & Montezuma Railroad (G&M) to connect the two communities of its corporate name. Montezuma, the seat of Poweshiek County, had been ignored by major roads that operated within the county and gladly supported and carried a tax proposal giving $55,000 to G&M, contingent only upon its construction from Grinnell. In the fall of 1875, the road pushed its rails toward Montezuma from a point on the Central south of Grinnell. Service between the two communities began on December 15. When completed, G&M operated fourteen miles of road, although it owned only one secondhand locomotive, one coach, and one coal car. It used the

Central's track from Grinnell to G&M Junction, rented terminal facilities at Grinnell, and was generally thought to be part of the larger road. Trains left Grinnell daily at 9:10 a.m. and 3:50 p.m., and left Montezuma for return trips at 11:25 a.m. and 6:00 p.m.[4]

Josiah Grinnell also had formulated plans to build a branch to State Center, northwestward from Newburg, a Central station six miles north of Grinnell. After gathering commitments for aid along the proposed line to serve Laurel and Van Cleve as well as State Center, J. B. Grinnell had relinquished his interest to former governor Samuel Merrill and his brother, J. H. Merrill. These two men then had gained the backing of Russell Sage and eventually built the twenty-six-mile line. There is some question as to the corporate linkage of this branch, if any, with the Grinnell & Montezuma road. G&M, however, had been operating for more than five years prior to the building of the line to

State Center, and it appears that the two entities were autonomous. Despite Grinnell's earlier solicitation, the feeder from Newburg to State Center was financed basically, if not entirely, by Merrill and Sage. The line entered service by early 1882.[5]

Central Iowa on its own fostered incorporation of the Iowa Central & Northwestern Railway (IC&NW) on October 5, 1880. This company was charged with building a thirty-four-mile branch from Minerva Junction (slightly over four miles northwest of Marshalltown) to Story City via Marietta, Minerva, Clemmons Grove, St. Anthony, Zearing, McCallsburg, and Roland. The northern portion of Story County was sadly lacking in railroad facilities at the time, and the affected townships gladly voted three or four mill levies designed to raise money to induce Iowa Central & Northwestern to build the line. IC&NW bought the necessary right-of-way and completed the road to Story City by December 1881.[6]

Figure 7.2. Mixed trains such as this one at St. Anthony were a regular feature on Central Iowa's branches. Vaughn R. Ward collection.

Iowa Central & Northwestern also was authorized to build a feeder line from Hampton to Belmond. Construction of this 22.5-mile line incorporated a dormant grade thrown up in 1872 by a now defunct road with the heady-sounding name Iowa Pacific. The "Pacific" had fallen into the hands of the Dubuque & Dakota Railroad, from which the Iowa Central & Northwestern eventually purchased a part of the property, but the circumstances surrounding this purchase were dubious. Indeed, IC&NW "jumped the claim" of Dubuque & Dakota the day after that company's lease expired (November 1, 1880). The Dubuque company had ordered its men to work on the grade until the lease expired, and they had done so. On the very night the contract expired, however, IC&NW crews started building the branch northwestward from Hampton under cover of darkness. The Dubuque crews soon appeared and immediately attempted to tear out the tracks just put in place by the Central's men. Skirmishes followed. In the end, IC&NW emerged a somewhat inglorious victor.[7]

Townships along the way voted aid to help this company—"provided the road was completed and an engine run [to Belmond] by November 1, 1881." Yet 1881 was not good for railroad building because weather conditions conspired to impede progress. Work crews struggled to get track down through Latimer and Alexander and were in sight of Belmond by the latter part of October; however, a large slough remained to be crossed. Farmers of the area saved the day. As one observer later recalled, they "hauled straw and hay into the slough and plowed up sod to lay on top upon which to place the ties." It proved to be a dangerously soft but passable roadbed. In the end, "locomotive No. 11, in charge of Engineer Win McClure . . . opened its steam throat, and for the first time in the history of [Belmond] sent shrill screams up and down the rich Iowa valley and across [the] rolling prairies."[8]

A celebration was called for, and a huge barbecue featuring roast oxen was held, followed by games, speeches, and other forms of excitement. Special trains from Ackley, Rockwell, Hampton, and Sheffield added large contingents of well-wishers for the festive occasion. The editor of the *Belmond Herald* understated reality when he reported: "Belmond has the iron horse and we are all happy."[9]

Figure 7.3. The Central's management bet on feeder business from branches. Business at Alexander, on the Belmond Branch, suggests that the Central's gamble paid off. Vaughn R. Ward collection.

Meanwhile, the New Sharon, Coal Valley & Eastern Railway Company had been chartered on January 29, 1880. The purpose of this company was to build a diagonal road from Newton southeastward to New Sharon, twenty-eight miles distant, with a short perpendicular stub from Lynnville Junction to Lynnville. The road was further authorized to continue its southeastward path—intersecting the Central at New Sharon—to Martinsburg, Brighton, and on to the Mississippi River. Work was started at New Sharon, with crews throwing up grades in both directions. The line to Newton eventually was opened as planned to serve Taintor, Lynnville Junction, Lynnville, Sully, Killduff, and Murphy, but after significant work had been done on the grade from New Sharon toward Martinsburg, that project was called off, and the starting point of the Mississippi River extension was moved southward to Oskaloosa. From that community the line would be built east to a junction with the original survey near Martinsburg, and then on to the eastern boundary of Iowa.[10]

The years 1880–82 constituted a period of significant secondary construction for Central Iowa; work was going forward on five separate projects at once. In 1882 Central Iowa decided to absorb all of these expansion projects. To facilitate sale of their State Center line to the Central, Russell Sage and Samuel Merrill changed its name to Keithsburg, Grinnell & Dakota Railway on February 28, 1882, then purchased Grinnell & Montezuma Railroad, which they merged into the new company. The next day, the deed to Keithsburg, Grinnell & Dakota (including the merged G&M) passed to Central Iowa, which also absorbed Iowa Central & Northwestern's Story City and Belmond branches at the same time.[11]

For whatever reason, Central Iowa did not immediately absorb New Sharon, Coal Valley & Eastern, which, incidentally, had changed its name to the more expansive-sounding Chicago, Burlington & Pacific (CB&P) on January 7, 1882. This company finished work on the Newton Branch by November 1.[12]

Meanwhile, as soon as graders finished their work on a specific portion of the new Oskaloosa–Mississippi River right-of-way, crews assigned to the construction train, under the direction of John Bray, pushed on with their work. Bray's crew, numbering two hundred men, had responsibility for putting down ties and laying rail. Each morning a locomotive was placed at the rear of four cars—three flatcars loaded with ties and one flatcar loaded

Figure 7.4. The expansive-sounding Chicago, Burlington & Pacific took responsibility for the Newton Branch as well as the extension eastward to the Mississippi River.

with rails—and headed for end-of-track, where the men were dropped off to take up their work. Strict division of labor was the rule, and each man had an assigned job for the day. Tie carriers moved cross ties on their shoulders to the spot where they were being lined up and readied for the rails. Next came rail carriers, then bolters, whose responsibility was to bind the rails together with angle bars, bolts, and nuts. Finally, spikers drove the rails fast to the ties. It was hard manual labor that pushed the line east toward the Mississippi River.[13]

During the construction season of 1882, as in the previous year, graders and track workers were plagued with bad weather and other adverse circumstances. When a new community was reached, however, the company ordinarily put together a special train and promoted a celebration. For instance, when the Central's rails reached Martins-burg during the summer of 1882, the company made up a train consisting of an engine, a flat-car, and a caboose, with the flatcar outfitted with benches for excursionists. Upon the train's arrival at Martinsburg, natives and guests alike listened to speeches by dignitaries, one of whom was the mayor of nearby Hedrick.[14]

Inclement weather was not the only variable hectoring Central Iowa. A narrow-gauge pike, Burlington & Western Railroad (B&W), had been incorporated on June 7, 1881, to connect Oskaloosa with Burlington & Northwestern Railroad, another narrow-gauge road, at Winfield. B&W and Chicago, Burlington & Pacific were located next door to one another much of the way from Winfield to Oskaloosa, seventy miles. Each company solicited funds from townships between the two points, and each predicted that the other

Figure 7.5. The mayor of Hedrick was delighted to be a speaker at the celebration honoring the railroad's arrival at nearby Martinsburg, but he was even more pleased when rails pushed into his community, which, as this view suggests, remained to be fully developed.

would not be built. (Burlington & Northwestern did try to sell itself to the Central in April 1882.) Accordingly, each surveyed a line of route assuming that the other company would become discouraged and subsequently drop out.[15]

To the contrary, both lines *were* built, and when the two construction companies met west of Brighton, the stage was set for an all-out battle. As the narrow-gauge crews went to work on the morning of April 13, 1882, they found that CB&P crews had worked during the night to build a track across their grade and right-of-way. B&W crews responded by tearing out the new track and putting down their own. After each company had torn out the other's track a few times, the B&W men "anchored" theirs by placing loaded cars on the disputed property and then posted guards to ward off nocturnal prowlers from CB&P. This convinced CB&P's management that the "slim gauge" meant business, and CB&P's standard-gauge survey was tactfully relocated to bypass that particular contested area. That was not the last scrap, however. As CB&P approached the western outskirts of Brighton, B&W attempted to keep its rival from entering that community by constructing a spur track where the standard-gauge company wanted to build, putting cars on this spur and chaining their wheels to the rails. Eventually a court order was issued in favor of CB&P, and the road built on through Brighton.[16]

Another "battle" was fought at the Skunk River crossing west of Coppock. Again the smaller road had secured a favored position, and the contest was on. By this time CB&P had lost all patience with its narrow-gauge rival, and on Saturday, June 10, the standard-gauge road assembled a large number of horses and men with the idea of driving the smaller force from the B&W grade. That night each company bivouacked its men on the grade facing the enemy. The next morning the CB&P men "captured" part of the grade, but failed to subdue the B&W employees. An armistice ultimately was agreed

to, and right-of-way and crossing questions were handed to the courts, which eventually gave both companies separate rights-of-way over the Skunk.[17]

By February 1, 1883, the line was complete from Oskaloosa to Morning Sun, eighty miles. Crews then hustled eastward another fifteen miles through Newport and Oakville to the west bank of the Mississippi River. The Chicago, Burlington & Pacific Railroad (and the Trunk Line Construction Company, to which the construction work had been let) handed over the completed property to Central Iowa later in the spring of 1883.[18]

At this juncture President Isaac M. Cate made a startling announcement: "The intention of Central Iowa Railway Company, after crossing the Mississippi River, [is] to strike in a northeasterly direction toward Chicago, Illinois." Why would a north-south railroad wish to become a horizontal axis carrier? Simple, said Cate: "The Central began and ended on the prairie, running north and south, while the current of trade is east and west." As a consequence, the "Central occupied the inferior and subordinate position of tributary." To remedy that problem, Cate's management had "resolved on establishing the Central in the commanding dimensions of an east and west trunk line, with the advantages of a north and south position."[19]

Cate, however, eventually had second thoughts about the proposed Chicago outlet. It was true that long-haul traffic would become a reality with such a line, especially for traffic originating at Central Iowa stations. But the road's proposed route to Chicago was long and circuitous at best. It was unlikely that CI could develop rates or schedules that would be able to compete effectively with those of any road currently in place. Furthermore, the Iowa company was in large part dependent on the various east-west roads for a high percentage of its traffic, and those horizontal carriers were almost invariably Chicago concerns. Building a rival line would surely alienate their affections, and they would likely terminate beneficial interchange

Figure 7.6. The Central and its upstart neighbor were nearly cheek to jowl at some locations, including Coppock, where both crossed the Skunk River. The Central's track is at right.

agreements. Because revenue derived from the proposed line would not match that lost from existing connections—and for other reasons—the Central's management gave up the Chicago proposal and directed its energies toward the procurement of another eastern terminal. Peoria became the new candidate, and Central Iowa immediately attempted to bring its influence to bear on the fledgling Peoria & Farmington Company (P&F).[20]

On February 27, 1837, the Illinois legislature had passed an act establishing a "General System of Internal Improvements" that included a line of standard-gauge railroad to be built westward from Peoria to Warsaw, a point on the Mississippi River. Work had been done on a grade west from Peoria in 1838, but construction had been suspended in favor of an alternate route. The grade eventually fell to the Peoria & Oquawka Company, but again it

was given up, and the state eventually took over the property. Indefinite postponement of the steamcar era was not an option, however; Illinois had too much to offer. Its agricultural potential was well recognized—rich topsoil "ten feet deep . . . fine as buckwheat flour . . . black as gunpowder," as one observer put it—and the annual value of its manufacturing output, especially farm machinery, meatpacking, and distilling, would shortly surpass that of its agriculture.[21]

The Peoria & Farmington Railroad had been organized on March 27, 1869, under a special charter granted by the Illinois legislature. No work had been done on the historic right-of-way west of Peoria, and it seems as if P&F promoters were simply making sure that they would have access to the property if the route could be fashioned into a real railroad.[22]

Meanwhile, efforts were being made at Keithsburg, an aspiring community northwest of Peoria on the Mississippi River, to incorporate a narrow-gauge company designed to build and operate a road from that place across the entire state of Illinois to the Indiana border (with a branch line to Chicago). This company, the Keithsburg & Eastern Railroad, had been organized on September 22, 1873. Its promoters had made this optimistic announcement: "It is proposed that this line shall be the Illinois Division of the Forty-First Parallel Railroad of the United States which is a line of road for cheap transportation now organized and to extend from New York to Omaha, on or near the forty-first parallel of latitude, with branches to the lakes and other commercial points." This was certainly an ambitious project for an organization that could, at that time, boast a grade of only eight miles, no iron, and no trains. Eventually the road did manage to grade eighteen miles to the east from Keithsburg, but it never turned a wheel.[23]

Another aspiring narrow-gauge company had been chartered by a special act of the Illinois legislature on October 16, 1875. This one, the Monmouth & Illinois River Railway, was to build from a point on the Mississippi across from Burlington, Iowa, through Monmouth and on east for a total of 130 miles. The company had 25 miles of grade and

60 miles of right-of-way purchased by the middle of 1880.[24]

About this same time, William Hanna and D. P. Phelps, both of Monmouth, elected to put life into the dormant Peoria & Farmington Railway, dubbed Poor & Friendless by some disrespectful wag. These two men had been active in the development of the Burlington, Monmouth & Illinois River Company, but now they turned their joint physical, mental, and financial resources toward energizing P&F. They quickly succeeded in acquiring a majority of its stock at 25 cents on the dollar, and in that fashion they gained control of the company.[25]

Much credit for the eventual completion of the Peoria road must be given to the dynamic and resourceful William Hanna. Born in Fayette County, Indiana, he succumbed to the 1849 gold fever and proceeded west to California driving an ox team. He did strike gold there, but returned to Monmouth, where he invested his money and engaged in farming, manufacturing, banking, and railroad building. It was Hanna who ultimately succeeded in gaining the capital necessary to build the line.[26]

Grading had started from Peoria in January of 1880, but construction moved slowly owing to the rugged terrain. It was not until May 13, 1880, that graders finally reached Maxwell, a little over four

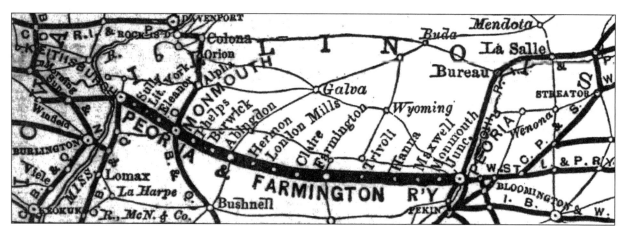

Map 7.2. Peoria & Farmington—dubbed Poor & Friendless by some disrespectful wag—would give Central Iowa entrance to Peoria and important connections there.

miles west of Peoria. Another contract was let at this point, and the graders moved on to finish the remaining fifteen miles to Farmington before the first snowfall.[27]

Hanna successfully negotiated a contract of acquisition with the owners of the Keithsburg & Eastern Railroad on February 22, 1881, and he was instrumental in gaining a deed from the Burlington, Monmouth & Illinois River Railroad on September 5, 1881. Even as he was busy buying up railroad charters, in June 1881 his own track workers pushed west beyond Maxwell. September 16 saw President Hanna entertain the Peoria County supervisors by taking them on a special train to the P&F railhead, at a point now called Hanna City. On the return trip, the supervisors stopped off at the Peoria County Poor Farm for the annual inspection of that institution. It must have been a rewarding day for Hanna, and for the supervisors as well.[28]

Scheduled passenger service from Peoria to Farmington, twenty-four miles, began on December 19, 1881, with morning and afternoon departures from each terminal. Now that regular service to Farmington had been initiated, Hanna was even more anxious to unite the newly acquired Keithsburg & Eastern and the Burlington, Monmouth & Illinois River with his favored Peoria & Farmington. As a result, early 1882 saw crews put down the line west of Farmington. By the end of the year, passenger service had been extended another twenty-five miles to Abingdon. Central Iowa supported all of this; indeed, on December 2, 1882, Peoria & Farmington changed its corporate title to Central Iowa Railway Company of Illinois.[29]

Only twenty-seven days into the new year, the "new" Central Iowa reached Monmouth and continued its westward thrust. Heavy snows and the resultant floods delayed the road, but on March 20, 1883, the first train rolled into Keithsburg, ninety miles from Peoria. Regular through service from

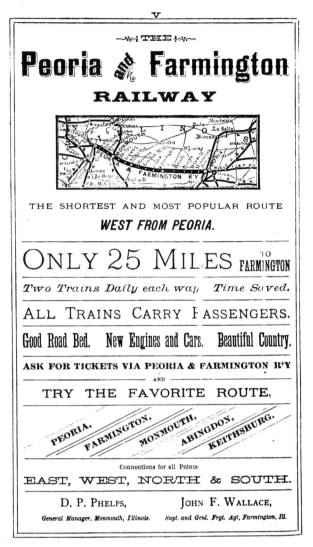

Figure 7.7. Peoria & Farmington proudly advertised itself in *Gould's Peoria City Directory* for 1882–83.

Peoria was not inaugurated, however, until some forty days later, when the company accepted delivery of the entire line from the contractors. Now all that separated Central Iowa's two east-west segments—from Oskaloosa to the Mississippi and from Keithsburg to Peoria—was the mighty Mississippi River. But it would be no mean task bridging that gap.[30]

Back when New Sharon, Coal Valley & Eastern agents had been moving from township to township enlisting aid to build that company's proposed line of road, two additional companies had been formed to bridge the Mississippi. The Mercer County Bridge Company had been incorporated on December 19, 1881, to build from the Illinois side, while the Keithsburg Bridge Company had been formed on December 26 to build from the Iowa side. These two companies were corporately linked and not rival concerns, so it had benefited both when on April 22, 1882, Congress had given the Mercer County Bridge Company permission to span the main channel of the Mississippi.[31]

Before a permanent bridge could be built, however, ferry service was established to handle through shipments. But expensive construction was necessary even to facilitate this. Consequently, on the Illinois side the Mercer County Bridge Company built an incline and approach, and on the Iowa side the Keithsburg Bridge Company built its own incline, spanning Black Hawk Chute and Black Hawk Island, opposite its Illinois counterpart.[32]

Car ferry service between the two states was scheduled to begin on October 11, 1883, and predictably there was a grand celebration at Keithsburg upon the arrival of an excursion train from Peoria that day. There was a hitch in the original plans, however, for regular operations did not actually commence until a few days later. This was of little matter, for Keithsburg was now an important terminal point on the new railroad.[33]

During the winter of 1884–85, a "winter bridge" was constructed about one thousand feet south of the site later used for the first steel bridge. It was obvious, of course, that this could be used only during the few months when the river was frozen over. And the ferry system itself was nothing more than a makeshift operation. Two vessels were employed—the *William Osborn,* a sternwheeler with a capacity of four cars, and later the *Golden Eagle,* a sidewheeler with a load limit of eight cars. All of these temporary means of transporting cars over the Mississippi proved burdensome as Central Iowa's traffic volume increased. In time the parent company brought pressure against its captive

bridge companies—neither of which, in the estimation of the Central's management, had been moving swiftly enough to bridge the river—to finish the job. Consequently, the Mercer County Bridge Company was changed to the Keithsburg Bridge Company (of Illinois) on April 6, 1885, and the Keithsburg Bridge Company (of Iowa) was deeded over to the new Illinois company on May 13, 1885. The officers of the new firm were William Hanna, president; G. E. Taintor, vice president; Alfred Sully, treasurer; and D. P. Phelps, secretary.[34]

The first piling for a permanent structure was driven on July 14, 1885; the bridge was completed by the Phoenix Bridge Company of Phoenixville, Pennsylvania, on February 22, 1886. It featured a 365-foot span, eight through trusses, a 742-foot timber trestle approach from the east, and a 965-foot timber trestle approach from the west. Central Iowa hired men to maintain this impressive structure although ownership remained vested in the Keithsburg Bridge Company.[35]

So it was that Central Iowa joined an exclusive group of railroads that had bridged the Mississippi River. In the beginning, traffic was light over the Peoria extension, and it was generally perceived only as a strategic branch. Little by little, however, traffic representatives convinced more and more shippers of the value of routing their shipments over the Peoria line. Terminal interchanges at Peoria were much less crowded than those at Chicago, and shippers could save a number of hours—maybe even days—by routing in this manner. Now, too, vast deposits of coal had been discovered in Illinois along the line between Abingdon and Maxwell; voluminous if relatively short-haul traffic for the Central was the result.[36]

Even as Central Iowa was adding mileage during the early 1880s, it was also subtracting. The bulk of its northern business was interchanged with the Milwaukee Road at Mason City, leaving Central Iowa with a stub line from Mason City to Northwood. Revenues derived from the operation

Figure 7.8. As the permanent bridge across the Mississippi River was completed, many were probably asking: Would traffic on the Peoria extension justify the great expense of bridging the Mississippi?

of this segment were almost nil because Burlington, Cedar Rapids & Northern had gained permission from the state regulatory agency to compete with Central Iowa for local traffic on the Central's own trackage between Manly Junction and Northwood. In sum, the Cedar Rapids concern was a strong competitor, and the Central was losing money on the operation of its stub line. Therefore, in August 1880 President Cate ordered that operation of Central trains be halted north of Manly Junction. Then he leased the Northwood line to BCR&N as sole operator. Although this arrangement was acceptable to both railroad companies, Worth County quickly complained to Iowa's Board of Railroad Commissioners. After a lengthy investigation, the commissioners demanded that the Central restore service. The order was ignored for a long while, but eventually BCR&N and Central Iowa did agree to an arrangement whereby revenues and expenses would be shared in an equitable way. Nevertheless, the Cedar Rapids company retained the bulk of the traffic. Indeed, Central Iowa operated only a turn-around mixed train (one handling both passengers and freight) from Mason City to Northwood.[37]

On the southern end of the main line, expan-sion had been discouraged by the loss of the "old" Iowa Central grade to Coatesville. And the bad news continued. Building the Missouri, Iowa & Nebraska Railroad (MI&N) into Centerville from the southeast, coupled with construction of its sponsored Centerville, Moravia & Albia Railroad (CM&A) connecting the communities in that corporate name, fully curtailed any expansion south on the part of Central Iowa. The driving force behind these two new southeast Iowa companies was Francis M. Drake, who had grown up in that corner of the state but had yielded to gold fever during the early 1850s. He later returned to Iowa and joined the Union Army to serve in the Civil War, emerging as a brevet brigadier general. Subsequently he entered the law profession, practicing at Centerville before becoming active in railroading. In 1873 he had been responsible for building the Centerville, Alexandria & Nebraska City Railroad (the predecessor of MI&N) into Centerville from Alexandria, Missouri. This road crossed the St. Louis–Ottumwa line of the St. Louis, Kansas City & Northern Railroad at Glenwood Junction, Missouri, just south of the Iowa border. Drake's objectives for the MI&N were manifold, but his primary desire was to extend the line west toward the Missouri River, a mission that was accomplished in later years.[38]

Possibly to forestall forever the building of Central Iowa into MI&N's service area, Drake had been granted a charter to build the Centerville, Moravia & Albia on May 6, 1879. That road had been constructed in 1880 from Centerville to Albia, with General Drake (later to become governor of Iowa) announcing that Albia was merely a stopping point on that road's drive to the Iowa state capital. Further growth for CM&A, however, was negated by powerful Chicago, Burlington & Quincy, which already had built a line beyond Albia into the proposed area of expansion ahead of the Centerville company. Moreover, Jay Gould wished to drive into the same region and tap Des Moines with his Wabash, St. Louis & Pacific (successor to St. Louis, Kansas City & Northern). With Gould looking over his shoulder, Drake's company agreed to handle Gould's trains over its tracks as soon as the Gould-sponsored Des Moines & St. Louis Railway was completed from Albia to Des Moines in 1882. By this arrangement, a passenger from St. Louis would ride over Gould's Wabash, St. Louis & Pacific Railroad to Glenwood Junction, thence over the rails of Drake's MI&N to Centerville and over

Drake's Centerville, Moravia & Albia to Albia to gain the rails of Gould's Des Moines & St. Louis for the trip on to the Iowa capital. The Drake roads and the Gould roads both were friendly to Central Iowa—reflecting, most likely, the influence of Russell Sage on Jay Gould and the influence of both men on General Drake.[39]

When the Central Iowa Railway had taken over the assets of the Central Railroad Company of Iowa in 1879, it had inherited about two hundred miles of line and twenty-four locomotives. Six years later, however, the company was operating about five hundred miles of line and fifty-seven locomotives, including a number of engines leased from other roads. The long-standing policy of naming locomotives ended during the early 1880s. Thereafter only those engines assigned to paycar trains and directors' specials retained names. Most memorable of all Central power, as far as the road's employees were concerned, was Number Ten, a majestic "standard" (4-4-0) engine with red-rimmed drivers, a fine-sounding chime whistle, and a gold eagle perched atop the sand dome. The "Ten Spot," originally named *I. M. Cate* and later christened *Russell Sage*, was traditionally assigned to pull the paymaster as he made his way from station to station. Whenever

Figure 7.9. Central Iowa's *Charles Alexander* was a marvelous example of the locomotive builders' art, but among employees the favorite was the *Russell Sage,* which was assigned to paycar duties.

employees heard the sweet sounds of the *Russell Sage*'s whistle, all work came to a halt and men jostled for position in the pay line.[40]

Equally important was the company's rolling stock. In 1880, Central Iowa had owned 10 passenger cars and 9 mail, baggage, and express cars, but by 1885 it had doubled the equipment used in passenger service. It was much the same in terms of the freight inventory. The company owned 625 freight cars in 1880 and owned or leased 1,588 freight cars in 1895.

Table 7.1 Breakdown of the Central's rolling stock, 1880 and 1885

Year	Boxcars	Stock cars	Flat and coal cars	Company cars	Total
1880	314	30	279	2	625
1885	250★	60	300★	22	1,558

Source: Poor's Manual of the Railroads, *1880 and 1885.*
★ *Leased.*

Other statistics mirrored Central Iowa's physical growth. The company had only 600 employees in 1880, but in 1885 required the services of 1,110. Revenues likewise increased. Passenger receipts had been $217,792 in 1880, but were $280,950 in 1885. Freight operations had garnered $636,472 in 1880 against receipts of $1,026,628 in 1885. (In terms of tonnage handled, coal was far and away the greatest contributor, followed by grain, merchandise, livestock, and lumber.) Total revenues similarly increased, from $883,000 in 1880 to $1,333,568 in 1885, opposed to operating expenses of $538,145 in 1880 and $982,338 in 1885.

Numbers alone did not define the company or its reputation. During the 1870s, someone long lost to history had nicknamed the Central the "Hook & Eye." Just how that moniker was derived is not certain. Frank P. Donovan Jr., author of *Mileposts on the*

Figure 7.10. A large number of men and boys gathered near the Marshalltown shops in front of what may have been the company paycar. Vaughn R. Ward collection.

Figure 7.11. By the time this photo of Central Iowa's 4-4-0 engine 18 was made at the Marshalltown scale house, the former road engine had been relegated to yard duty. Note the lanterns hung beneath the headlight as well as the crude link-and-pin coupling. Central Iowa was slow to embrace modern automatic couplers; cost was the issue. Vaughn R. Ward collection.

Table 7.2. Total freight tonnage as a percentage of the total, by sector of commodity, 1880 and 1885

Commodity	1880	1885
Agriculture	23.0	10.4
Mines	54.7	73.4
Forests	6.4	4.0
Manufacturing	1.0	NA
Merchandise	9.0	8.1
Other	8.9	4.1

Source: Poor's Manual of the Railroads, *1880 and 1885.*
Note: *NA = not available.*

Prairie, theorized, however, that it came from the company's monogram. Said Donovan: "On the title page of a schedule of 1874 vintage, when the line was called Central Railroad Company of Iowa, is a large I with two smaller R's having their straight line in the I. A C is placed on its back across the top of the I. The C is the hook and the I the eye!"[41]

Hook & Eye obviously was an unusual "handle," and the road became widely known as such when travelers carried the road's nickname across the country. Even more important in this regard were the countless "boomers" whom Donovan labeled "those itinerant railroaders of yesterday who went from road to road." These men found a haven on the "Hook," for the Iowa road often was in financial doldrums and forced to hire almost anybody who happened along. By the same token, itinerants sought employment on the Central as a last resort due to its normally poor wages and always poor working conditions. Consequently, it was unusual to see the same train crew twice. As these men moved about the country,

Figure 7.12. The Central's "Hook & Eye" logo featured a prominent *I* to emphasize Iowa, with smaller *R*s representing "railroad" in the corporate name and the *C* standing for "Central"—the "hook" attached to the "eye."

they reminisced about the "Hook," and the road grew to be famous—or infamous, depending on how the road was remembered.[42]

The Central's customers were of similarly divided opinion, but there was no question that the railroad was at the core of every on-line community. New Sharon, twelve miles north of Oskaloosa, was typical. The railroad's arrival in 1871 had ushered in a veritable boom. By 1878, New Sharon boasted three hotels, blacksmith shops, grocery stores, drugstores, and drygoods stores; two hardware stores and carriage makers; and one lumberyard, jewelry store, bakery, bank, livery, and grinding mill. It also had eight lawyers, four doctors, and the *Sharon Star* newspaper. There were six churches, a large concert hall stood at the corner of Main and Market, and private and public schools flourished. The depot—at East Depot and South Railroad Streets—was an especially active place, particularly after the Newton Branch was completed in 1882.[43]

The Central always was a local road catering to local needs and interests. There were some very important connections along the route, however, and passengers and freight moved in all directions from these junction points. For example, the Iowa road operated through trains to Ottumwa via the Burlington & Missouri River connection at Albia in its earliest days, but this arrangement was canceled shortly after its inception, and subsequently trains operated to Ottumwa via Eddyville and the Keokuk & Des Moines Railroad, a procedure in force off and on for a number of years. Through service to St. Paul/Minneapolis operated via Chicago, Milwaukee & St. Paul at Mason City. For example, in 1874 travelers were able to leave St. Paul at 6:40 a.m., pause very briefly at Austin for a meal, and then reboard the train for Mason City. Arrival at Mason City was advertised at 3:00 p.m. Here the Central attached a through car from the Twin Cities to its *Kansas City Express*. The *Express* was scheduled to reach Ackley at 4:57 p.m. and Marshalltown at 6:50 p.m., where passengers were given "twenty minutes for supper" and a Pullman sleeping car was added to the train's consist. The *Express* was scheduled to reach Grinnell at 8:20 p.m. and Eddyville at 10:30 p.m. There Keokuk and St. Louis passengers were transferred to cars of the Keokuk & Des Moines road. Finally, the *Express* was advertised to arrive at Albia Union Station at 11:30 p.m., affording connections for both east and west via Burlington & Missouri River's "Atlantic and Pacific Express Trains." The Pullman that the Central had brought down from Marshalltown continued on its way to Kansas City.[44]

By June 1878 the Central had made agreements with St. Louis, Kansas City & Northern for passenger operations from St. Paul to St. Louis and Kansas City. To be sure, passengers previously had been able to travel over the same routes to these cities, but now "through" trains were available, eliminating the need to change cars. Under this agreement, Milwaukee Road hauled the cars from

St. Paul to Mason City, where delivery was made
to the Central, which hurried passengers through
the Hawkeye State before delivering them to St.
Louis, Kansas City & Northern at Ottumwa, as the
Central then had trackage rights over Keokuk &
Des Moines from Eddyville to Ottumwa. Passengers could leave St. Paul on train 2, the *Kansas
City Express,* at 6:10 a.m., and arrive in St. Louis at
6:15 p.m. the following day. Or they could leave on
train 4, the *St. Louis Express,* at 6:25 p.m., arriving in St. Louis at 7:10 a.m. a day and a half later.
Both of these trains made connections at Moberly
with the Kansas City–bound trains of the St. Louis,
Kansas City & Northern. Northbound service was
much the same, with two daily trains departing
from their respective terminals about twelve hours
apart. While every train provided coaches, trains
3 and 4 also boasted "Pullman's Finest Drawing
Room Palace Cars Every Day of the Month." Of
course all trains stopped for meals; train 1 paused
for lunch at Sheffield, trains 2 and 3 for dinner at
Marshalltown, and train 4 for breakfast at Sheffield
and lunch at Grinnell.[45]

The year 1886 witnessed a number of innovations. One major change brought a traffic agreement with A. B. Stickney's new Minnesota &
Northwestern Railroad (M&NW). This company
recently had completed a line from St. Paul to
Austin and through Lyle to Manly Junction, giving
Central Iowa a much desired second connection to
the north. The Iowa company immediately leased
the Manly Junction–Lyle, Minnesota, segment from
M&NW and operated trains to that point. Considerable freight and passenger business still went
to CM&StP at Mason City, of course, but the
Central's primary traffic allegiance during these
few years was with Minnesota & Northwestern.[46]

Additional changes for the year 1886 included
the operation of drawing-room sleeping cars on
M&NW and on the Central's Minneapolis-to-
Peoria through run. At Peoria the sleeper was
handed to an eastern carrier for the remainder of

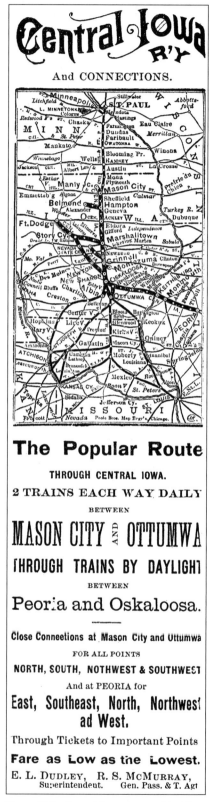

Figure 7.13. Central Iowa postured itself as
the "Popular Route," and indeed it offered
a multitude of connections favoring local
patrons.

its trip to Columbus, Ohio. Even more noteworthy was the Marshalltown–Chicago sleeper routing that saw a handsome Woodruff car leave Marshalltown each day for Keithsburg and a connection there with Chicago, Burlington & Quincy. From that point the sleeper made its way along Burlington's Galva Branch until the main line was reached and the car was safely deposited in the care of an express train for the last few miles of its lengthy journey to Chicago. One final change in passenger routings for 1886 occurred on the southern end of the main line when the Central's passenger department decided to operate through St. Louis cars via Oskaloosa and Hedrick (on the Peoria line), and down to Ottumwa over a CM&StP branch. There the cars were delivered to Wabash, St. Louis & Pacific (successor to St. Louis, Kansas City & Northern), which simply picked up the train twenty miles east of the former junction at Albia. Needless to say, several of these innovations were implemented on a trial basis and passed quickly.[47]

Meanwhile, freight service was provided by six trains working each way along the line be-tween Mason City and Oskaloosa every business day. From Oskaloosa to Peoria, two freights each way per day handled all but variable coal traffic on the Peoria extension. Two daily-except-Sunday mixed trains operated on the Newton, Belmond, and Montezuma branches. Business on the State Center Branch warranted only one daily-except-Sunday round-trip for the mixed train on that line, and Story City was the recipient of a daily-except-Sunday mixed train with the exception of Fridays, when traffic warranted two round-trip "accom-modation trains" in lieu of the usual mixed train. Although travelers did not have much choice on the branches, they could ride almost all freight trains on the main line simply by purchasing a coach ticket and presenting it to the conductor.[48]

Throughout this period, Oskaloosa was really the hub of operations. For a while train crews worked from Oskaloosa all the way to Mason City and even through to Peoria, although crew-change points eventually were established at Keithsburg (later moved to Monmouth) and Marshalltown. Additional shops were established at Oskaloosa, and

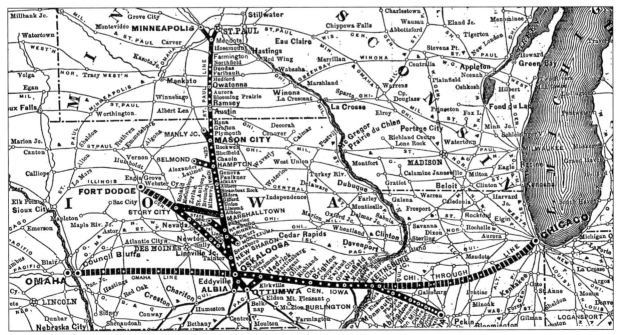

Map 7.3. Was Central Iowa serious about driving a line to Council Bluffs and another to Chicago? If so, it certainly would have created a strangely configured route structure—however beneficial to Oskaloosa.

··· THE ···

CHICAGO AND CENTRAL IOWA

NEW

• Through Car Line •

RUNNING OVER THE

CHICAGO, BURLINGTON & QUINCY

◄ AND ►

CENTRAL IOWA R'YS,

Via KEITHSBURG and OSKALOOSA.

Pullman Sleeping Car between Chicago and Oskaloosa,
and Day Coach between Chicago and Lyle, Minn.

The Quickest and most Direct Line between

CHICAGO and MORNING SUN,	MARSHALLTOWN,
WINFIELD,	ELDORA,
BRIGHTON,	ACKLEY,
HEDRICK,	HAMPTON,
OSKALOOSA,	MASON CITY, IA.,
GRINNELL,	and LYLE, MINN.

Close Connections made at CHICAGO with all Lines to and from the East.

THROUGH TICKETS AND BAGGAGE CHECKS TO ALL POINTS

EAST, WEST, NORTH, AND SOUTH.

Figure 7.14. Surely one of the most curious Pullman car routes was between Oskaloosa and Chicago via Keithsburg. It suggested that Central Iowa was part of an innovative tradition in the passenger-carrying trade.

dispatchers' offices were established there. Passengers took a great liking to the massive Blackstone Hotel across the tracks from the depot, and over the years hundreds of local citizens found employment at the railroad. Oskaloosa's position of prominence would have been further solidified had the Central's plans to become a prominent east-west carrier been carried through to fruition, for Oskaloosa was in line to be the pivot where the existing line from Northwood to Albia would bisect a projected line westward to Council Bluffs and the completed line to Peoria (with a projected line jutting off to Chicago at Keithsburg). Surely it would have been the Hook & Eye's headquarters city if all that had come to pass.[49]

Incidentally, Central Iowa's management was heartily offended by the Hook & Eye nickname that had come to the road from the Central Railroad Company of Iowa. Consequently, in 1887 the company's passenger agents were instructed to give the road a new epithet, "The Marshalltown Route," and at the same time they promoted a fresh company nickname, "The Handy Line." Although both of these were appropriate, neither the new epithet nor the new nickname caught on. In the public's mind, Central Iowa remained the Hook & Eye.[50]

Among the Central's officers, Isaac M. Cate served as president until 1883, when Alfred Sully was elected. Sully, whose name often had been associated with construction companies owing close allegiance to the Central, served as president for only one year before being replaced by Elijah Smith. Under Smith, Central Iowa made more money in 1884 than in any other year to date. With the opening of the various branches and the Peoria extension, the Central's managers expected that revenues would climb. They likewise anticipated that operating expenses and taxes would increase. All of these expectations came true. But it was the fate of Smith to announce in October 1884 that expenses and revenues had risen unequally. The road, he observed, had earned insufficient income

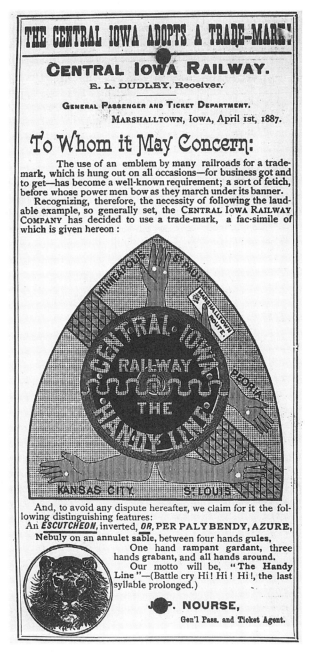

Figure 7.15. Central Iowa managers bridled at the "Hook & Eye" nickname, proposing instead "The Handy Line." The new idea did not take.

and would be forced to default on all but main line bonds. Revenues and expenses were down only slightly in 1885, and the net deficit increased. The year 1886 saw revenue and operating expenses up marginally over the previous year.[51]

In 1886 the annual meeting of shareholders was held in June, and a group of disenchanted stockholders chose to replace Elijah Smith with A. B. Stickney, who had been a schoolteacher, then a lawyer, and finally a railroad builder. Stickney had gained important notice when he had completed his Minnesota & Northwestern in 1885, and it was not surprising when the new president changed the Central's northern traffic patterns to feed his M&NW, leasing the new track of that company from Manly Junction to Lyle, Minnesota, to Central Iowa.[52]

For that matter, Stickney was among many who considered acquisition of the Central during this time. "Mr. Stickney is said to be on the eve of consolidating the Kansas City [Chicago, St. Paul & Kansas City, successor to Minnesota & Northwestern, and predecessor to Chicago Great Western] with Central Iowa," said one report from Minneapolis. Rock Island had taken a serious look at Central Iowa in 1880, Russell Sage had tried to tease Chicago & North Western into a lease, Milwaukee and Wabash had both expressed interest at varying times, and in 1885 the *Boston Transcript* reported flatly that Chicago, Burlington & Quincy would "assume control of Central Iowa." And for several years rumors had Chicago & Alton building from Lacon, Illinois, to connection with Central Iowa at Keithsburg, or Central Iowa building to connection with Chicago & Alton at Lacon.[53]

In any event, when Stickney assumed control of the Iowa road, the national economy was on the upswing after a short but sharp recession. On the surface, all looked well. But the Central had defaulted on interest payments since October 1884 and now had a net deficit of a quarter of a million dollars. By December 1, 1886, only five months after Stickney had taken office, the net deficit was up another quarter of a million and the road was thrown to the courts, with E. L. Dudley appointed as receiver.[54]

A. B. Stickney was a fine railroad man, and his want of success in bringing Central Iowa out of the red in 1886 cannot be attributed to his lack of interest or ability. It was more a matter of too much—if absolutely essential—expansion followed by a national recession. Nevertheless, the road was in adequate physical condition, its business was fairly well diversified, and the economy of the country was looking up. With good management by the receiver and with the dynamic energy of President Stickney, it should have been only a matter of time before the road was returned to its owners. Nevertheless, 1887 was a year of disaster for the road. Passenger and freight revenues were less than half of those for the previous year, and the Stickney-Dudley combination was forced to swallow hard as the road's bondholders contemplated reorganization of the company. To this end a new concern, the Iowa Railway Company, was incorporated on January 9, 1888, and was given a deed to the property by P. T. Lomax, special master, on July 24, 1888. The court then approved a plan that saw the Iowa Railway Company sell the property to yet another new firm—the Iowa Central Railway—on August 1. Iowa Central had been chartered in Illinois on May 14, 1888, under the careful tutelage of a bondholders' committee comprised of the omnipresent Russell Sage and long-time Central bondholders G. E. Taintor, Horace J. Morse, and others. Financial agreements included an exchange of Iowa Central securities for those of Central Iowa (of Iowa) and Central Iowa (of Illinois). In addition, bondholders and owners of capital stock were assessed $1.1 million for payment of the floating debt and the cost of reorganization. Formal transfer of the properties was delayed until May 16, 1889; E. L. Dudley was retained as receiver until that time.[55]

Iowa Central owners had gained respect for the abilities of Dudley, and as soon as his responsibilities as receiver were concluded, he was appointed general manager of the new company. Other officers included A. B. Stickney, president; Russell Sage, vice president; and Seth Zug, treasurer. The company headquarters remained in Marshalltown, where general manager Dudley kept close tabs on the five-hundred-mile Iowa Central Railway.[56]

THE

"HANDY LINE"

"The Tourist Route"

BETWEEN

ST. LOUIS, KANSAS CITY, ST. PAUL

AND

MINNEAPOLIS

This Through Line

COMPOSED OF THE

WABASH ST. LOUIS & PACIFIC,

CENTRAL IOWA,

MINNESOTA & NORTHWESTERN R'YS

Figure 7.16. During the Stickney years, Minnesota & Northwestern was the Central's favored partner to the north.

Chapter 8
IOWA CENTRAL RAILWAY

*Later when my father went braking on the Iowa Central . . . we moved to Keithsburg,
a sleepy town on the Mississippi River. Only it wasn't so sleepy then. It was a division point
on the Hook & Eye, as we called the Iowa Central. I used to like to watch the engines being
changed there. Those old high-wheeled American Standards fascinated me with their speed.
They were light, fast and smart. They pulled short trains with bantam-weight freight cars
and wooden open-platform day coaches with red-plush seats.*

—HUGH MCCARTHY, "I WAS BORN TO RAILROAD"

THE PROPERTY OF THE IOWA CENTRAL
Railway was turned over to President
A. B. Stickney in May 1889. He immediately took advantage of the company's
stable financial footing and the prosperity
of the times by placing an order for passenger and
freight equipment as well as seven locomotives. It

was to be Stickney's final contribution to
the Iowa Central, for at the first annual
meeting he was relieved of his assignment. In a highly unusual development,
Russell Sage, long associated with the
Iowa company in various capacities and long acknowledged to be the dominant force behind the

Figure 8.1. Stickney ordered newer power; humble switchers such as this one were soon to be shunting cars at Marshalltown, Oskaloosa, or Peoria.

74

Central's management, assumed the presidency in late 1889. As soon as Sage took office, he looked to the south and decided that it was time to bring one of his railroad "orphans" into the Iowa Central fold.[1]

Jay Gould interests had taken lease of the Centerville, Moravia & Albia Railroad during the early 1880s in order to facilitate movement of Wabash, St. Louis & Pacific Railway trains between St. Louis and Des Moines, and at Albia Central had been content to shunt its through trains over the Wabash/CM&A syndicate for movement to the south. With the decline of the Gould empire in 1885, however, the Centerville road had been set adrift and the Central had inaugurated an interchange with Wabash at Ottumwa. The derelict CM&A actually had ceased operation for a time, but when the Central was reorganized in 1889,

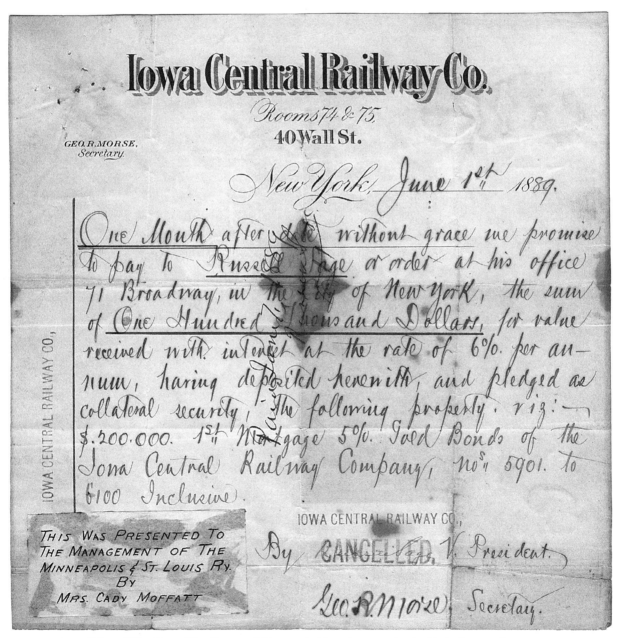

Figure 8.2. Russell Sage, "The Money King," payee of this note, had been long associated with the Iowa road.

a close kinship was established between the two concerns. Russell Sage undoubtedly was the prime mover in leasing CM&A to Iowa Central.[2]

Although legal commitments were not implemented until May 3, 1893, Iowa Central commenced its operation of the Centerville road effective August 12, 1889. The Central immediately cleaned up the dormant property and initiated movement of its trains to the Appanoose County seat, with Centerville, Moravia & Albia (reorganized April 1, 1890, as the Albia & Centerville Railway or A&C) receiving a fixed price per train mile. Iowa Central finally had shoved its railhead a few miles farther south, but the move was of little immediate significance because Wabash, St. Louis & Pacific (soon reorganized as the Wabash Railroad) connections were still made at Ottumwa.[3]

Under President Stickney, traffic arrangements had favored Minnesota & Northwestern at Lyle, Minnesota. M&NW was, of course, Stickney's own special project, and Iowa Central had leased the M&NW line between Manly Junction and Lyle soon after its completion. This cost about $8,000 per annum, but allowed longer hauls from which the road derived sufficient additional revenue to justify it. With Stickney's departure, however, the arrangement predictably was terminated; on January 31, 1890, the Manly Junction–Lyle property was returned to its owner. In another agreement between the two roads, the Central had leased its nine-mile line between Mason City and Manly Junction to M&NW; this contract was similarly ended on February 9, 1891, and the property restored to Iowa Central. With termination of these arrangements between the Sage and Stickney roads, Iowa Central again interchanged the bulk of its northern traffic with Chicago, Milwaukee & St. Paul at Mason City.[4]

The country was favored by good times during the first three years of the 1890s, and the Sage administration saw to it that the Central's property was at least adequately groomed. Indeed, the road

was keeping itself well ordered while at the same time moving freight and passengers with, for it, unparalleled efficiency. Business was so good, in fact, that the road declared a 1 percent dividend on preferred stock on April 10, 1892. Unfortunately, such prosperity was short-lived.[5]

The poor times of the mid-1890s did not appreciably affect operations of the Iowa company, although its earnings did fluctuate significantly. During the panic of 1893, the company's management kept the road out of bankruptcy only by using previously earned surplus, allowing maintenance to deteriorate, failing to purchase additional equipment, and generally applying policies of retrenchment. Times were difficult, but the road survived.

In an age of more leisurely travel, the Iowa Railroad Commissioners noted in 1893 that the average speed of Iowa Central passenger trains was twenty-five miles per hour, slightly lower than that of other Iowa roads but fast enough for most patrons of that age. However, the nature of Iowa Central's route structure precluded any large earnings from passenger operation, for despite the role it played in joint St. Paul–St. Louis service, Iowa Central was used primarily by patrons wishing passage to points up and down the line or by those who wished to use the local road only long enough to reach key east-west junction points. In 1893, for instance, the average distance traveled by its passengers was a mere 22.83 miles. Nevertheless, the company did haul well over a half million passengers in 1893, charging an average fare of .0253 cents per mile.[6]

Traffic arrangements (except during the brief

Figure 8.3. Iowa Central paid its bills, paid interest on its bonds, and even declared a small dividend.

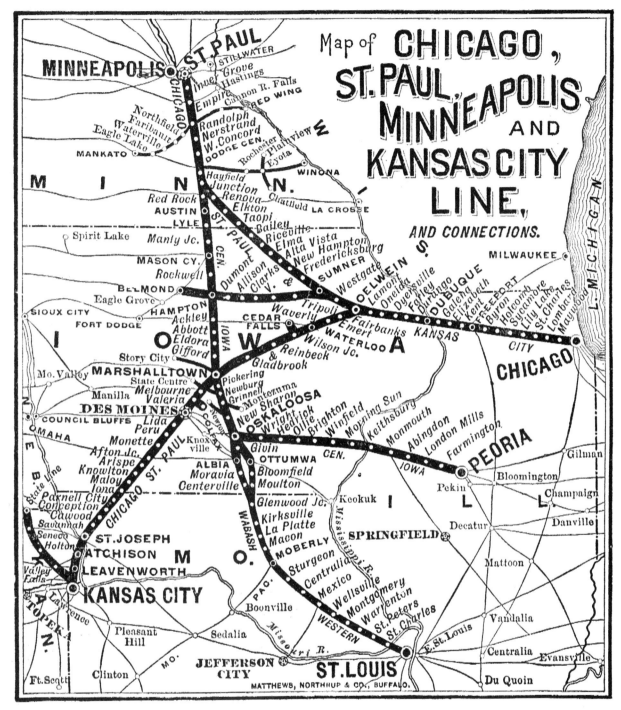

Map 8.1. Stickney's Minnesota & Northwestern eventually evolved into Chicago Great Western, but before that time he showed Central Iowa as an integral part of his own road.

Stickney era) were much the same as they had been for years. CM&StP handled business between the Twin Cities and Mason City Junction; Wabash moved the cars between Ottumwa and St. Louis.

In 1890, Iowa Central made a splash at Mason City, however, when it delivered "the first vestibule train that ever entered" the city—this representing St. Paul–St. Louis service—with "new coaches, palace sleeping cars and buffet cars." By mid-decade, Iowa Central's *Peoria Express,* also handling "palace sleeping cars," was given equal billing with the traditional *Kansas City–St. Louis Express.* The Peoria train left Minneapolis at 4:00 p.m. and arrived at Peoria at 10:00 a.m. the following day. The Kansas City–St. Louis train, featuring through "Day Coaches and Pullman Palace Buffet Sleeping Cars," departed from CM&StP's Minneapolis depot at 8:25 a.m. It was handed to Wabash at Ottumwa at 9:15 p.m. and arrived in Kansas City at 7:00 a.m. or in St. Louis at 7:25 a.m. Iowa Central picked up 33.8 percent of revenue on St. Paul–Kansas City tickets, 29.8 percent on St. Paul–St. Louis business. The Peoria train, incidentally, advertised "unexcelled dining car service," and the menu was truly splendid, including oxtail soup (25¢), raw oysters (40¢ per half dozen), a large porterhouse steak (65¢), calves' liver and bacon (35¢), stewed potatoes in cream (10¢), asparagus tips (15¢), a boiled tongue

sandwich (10¢), cream toast (20¢), and wheat cakes with maple syrup (15¢), as well as "game, vegetables and fruits in their season." To be sure, the menu offered an astonishing fifty-nine items. Oh yes, "bread, butter and potatoes [were] served with all hot meals free." There were no such marvelous culinary opportunities on accommodation trains, of course, although Iowa Central pledged to provide "elegant day coaches" on locals; these trains and all others without dining car service paused at "meal stops" for the benefit of passengers and crew alike.[7]

Elsewhere, in 1896 the Oskaloosa–Albia–Centerville line was served by three daily-except-Sunday round-trips. The same year, daily-except-Sunday mixed ("hog and human") train service was offered on all branches. The road's passenger service reached its zenith during the 1890s, when passenger agents publicized the route as "'The Short Line' between St. Paul, Minneapolis, Kansas City, Peoria

Figure 8.4. The average distance traveled by an Iowa Central patron in 1893 was 22.8 miles. Some of those miles were rolled up by persons riding branch line trains such as this one about to depart from Story City.

Figure 8.5. Train 1 had made its station stop at Sheffield at 12:25 p.m. and was bounding off for Rockwell and Mason City, where the equipment would be returned to Albia as train 2. Vaughn R. Ward collection.

and the Pacific Coast." Nevertheless, Iowa Central remained basically a local road catering to the transportation needs of local people and local products.[8]

Those needs were mostly homely and routine, with an occasional exception. In 1872, a terrible fire at Marshalltown brought anguished cries for help, to which the railroad responded by rushing the Grinnell Hook & Ladder Company up the line with an emergency run that consumed a bare thirty-four minutes for the twenty-five-mile trip. Later on, a woman from Hampton who taught at a trackside rural school near Faulkner was delivered each Monday by an obliging crew making an unscheduled stop, and she was retrieved each Friday by another helpful crew. Special movements included excursions to the inviting banks of the Iowa River at Union and Steamboat Rock; from Montezuma

over the Grinnell & Montezuma and from the State Center Branch to the Poweshiek County Fair at Grinnell; to Peoria and to Keithsburg for steamboat trips on the Mississippi River; to Marshalltown for dedication of the new courthouse; and to Coppock for picnics at Trite's Park, along with swimming, boating, and even trips up the Skunk River on a small steam launch. In 1899 the Buffalo Bill Show drew a huge crowd to Marshalltown off the Story City Branch. Regular trains were jammed for holidays; Iowa Central had no reserve equipment, and crowding was inevitable. For example, about two hundred eager patrons at Gilman were dismayed when an already overloaded northbound train arrived at that station, but they piled aboard anyway, taking standing-room-only refuge in the baggage car. "The Fourth of July this year was the same on

IOWA CENTRAL RAILWAY.

PEOPLE OF THE NORTHWEST WHO CONTEMPLATE GOING

Eastward

SHOULD REMEMBER THAT THE

Iowa Central Railway

is the most direct line via **Peoria**

READ THE TIME TABLE:

	Daily	Ex. Sun.
Lv. Minneapolis.........	4:30 p. m.	....
" St. Paul.......	4:40 p. m.	....
" Mason City.........	10:05 p. m.	6:25 a. m.
" Marshalltown.......	1:25 a. m.	9:40 a. m.
" Grinnell	2:15 a. m.	10:30 a. m.
" Oskaloosa..........	3:25 a. m.	11:40 a. m.
Ar. Peoria	10:45 a. m.	6:35 p. m.
Lv. Peoria	11:40 a. m.	7:25 p. m.
Ar. Indianapolis, Ind....	6:05 p. m.	3:30 a. m.
" Cleveland, O........	1:50 a. m.	2:30 p. m.
" Cincinnati, O.......	9:05 p. m.	7:10 a. m.
" Washington, D. C....	3:39 p. m.	6:47 a. m.
" Philadelphia, Pa.....	8:00 p. m.	10:15 a. m.
" New York...........	10:30 p. m.	8:00 a. m.

Palace Sleeping Cars and Elegant Day Coaches, Minneapolis and St. Paul to Peoria and free Reclining Chair Cars, Mason City to Peoria. Compartment Sleeping and Parlor Cars, Peoria to Indianapolis and Cincinnati.

BUY YOUR TICKETS via PEORIA, ILL.

For maps, folders and all information, call upon coupon agent or address the

General Passenger and Ticket Agent,

IOWA CENTRAL RAILWAY,

MARSHALLTOWN, IOWA.

Figure 8.6. Iowa Central enthusiastically urged passengers to embrace routing through Peoria, and during the 1890s, in cooperation with Milwaukee Road, assigned premier equipment between Minneapolis and Peoria.

IOWA CENTRAL RAILWAY.

A PLEASING FEATURE

OF A TRIP OVER THE

IOWA CENTRAL ROUTE

IS THE

Unexcelled Dining Car Service

To be found on all passenger trains to and from Peoria, Ill. The dining cars are operated under the direction and personal supervision of one of the best caterers in the country.

MEALS SERVED A LA CARTE

A Sample Menu

FRUITS

SOUPS
WITH BREAD AND BUTTER

French Bouillon 25c   Oxtail 25c   Julienne 25c

OYSTERS

Half dozen, raw or stewed 40c, fried 50c
One dozen, raw or stewed 75c, fried 85c
Celery 5c

Grape Nuts and Cream 15c   Oat Meal and Cream 15c
Pickles 10c   Olives 10c, stuffed 10c   Chow Chow 10c

STEAKS

Small Steaks 35c   Porterhouse 45c   Large Porterhouse 65c
Minced Ham and Scrambled Eggs 35c
Vienna Sausage 25c   Broiled Ham 30c   Ham and Eggs 40c
Breakfast Bacon 30c   Calves' Liver and Bacon 35c

EGGS

Fried, Scrambled or Boiled 10c   Ham Omelet 30c
Cheese Omelets 30c, Plain Omelets 25c

POTATOES

Lyonnaise 10c   German Fried 10c   French Fried 10c
Stewed Potatoes in Cream 10c

MISCELLANEOUS

Asparagus Tips 15c   Peas 15c   Sugar Corn 15c   Succotash 15c
Stewed Tomatoes 15c   Baked Beans 25c

COLD DISHES
WITH BREAD AND BUTTER

Salmon 25c   Boiled Ham 25c   Sardines 25c   Boiled Tongue 25c

SANDWICHES

Ham 10c   Chicken 15c   Tongue 10c
Bread and Butter 10c   Bread and Milk 20c   Crackers and Milk 15c
Dry or Buttered Toast 10c   Cream Toast 20c   Pie 10c
Wheat Cakes with Maple Syrup 15c
Coffee 10c   Tea 10c   Chocolate 10c   Milk 10c   Cream 20c

PRESERVES, ETC.

Strawberries 20c   Apricots 20c   Cherries 20c   Pineapple 20c
Peaches 20c   Raspberries 20c   Figs in Syrup 20c

Bread, Butter and Potatoes Served with all Hot Meat Orders Free.
Choice Domestic and Imported Cigars 10c and 15c each.
Game, Vegetables and Fruits in their seasons.

Figure 8.7. Iowa Central was not far off the mark in identifying its dining car cuisine as "unexcelled."

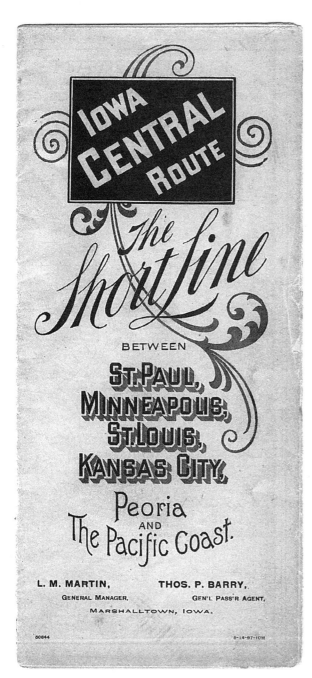

Figure 8.8. Iowa Central certainly was a player in the intercity trade, but its greatest contribution was in providing local service for local needs.

the Central as on all other public days and at all times, lack of proper accommodations for passengers," growled the editor of the local paper. "It was never known here to miss."[9]

There was no jeering or complaining but only cheering and admiration at Marshalltown in April 1898 when troops from Dubuque and Waterloo passed through town en route to the "splendid little war" with Spain. They were feted by veterans from the Iowa Soldiers Home and others, including Iowa Central personnel, who marched in a body to show their support and offer best wishes. A few days earlier, several hundred Iowa Central employees had appeared in front of the General Office Building with a new flag they had purchased to demonstrate patriotism, and general manager L. M. Martin was asked to raise it; he did so to great applause. And on May 2 Iowa Central joined other roads in dispatching special trains to Des Moines to cheer the men at Camp McKinley (the state fairgrounds) before they left for combat.[10]

In a few months the war was over and local attention turned again to the failures and foibles of Iowa Central. Late in November 1899, the conductor of a southbound passenger was left on the platform at Marshalltown when the engine men on the locomotive of his train mistook a signal meant for C&NW's *Colorado Special* on the adjacent track and highballed out of town without him. His absence was discovered before the train reached Dillon, seven miles distant, where it was held until the red-faced and highly agitated conductor could be delivered to his charge by light engine 104, which had been recruited for this emergency duty. The *Marshalltown Times-Republican* reported the incident in great detail and with mixed sentiments of bemusement and wonder.[11]

At the annual stockholders' meeting in 1898, a failing Russell Sage relinquished his duties as president and chairman of the board. Walking cane close at hand, now hard of hearing, the big, raw-boned

Figure 8.9. Iowa Central remained basically a local road catering to local needs. This view at McCallsburg on the Story City Branch implies as much. Vaughn R. Ward collection.

Figure 8.10. Iowa Central's chair car 86 was handsome enough, but the road simply had an insufficiency of such equipment to meet peak demand.

Figure 8.11. The engineer of Iowa Central's American Standard 4-4-0 engine 12 was about to get a roll on a passenger train out of Oskaloosa in this photo from 1897. Vaughn R. Ward collection.

Sage was replaced by Horace J. Morse, whose association with the concern went back to the days of the Central Railroad Company of Iowa. Although Sage had relinquished the obvious offices of power, the "Money King" nevertheless retained control over Iowa Central because he still held a position on the board of directors, a post that he retained until his death some years later.

Iowa Central always had been a prominent coal handler, and its importance as such increased during the 1890s. In 1898, a track was built from Albia to the mines at Hocking, a few miles south of the Monroe County seat, part of it over a grade created by the "old" Iowa Central in the mid-1860s. Eventually this same grade had fallen to Chicago, Burlington & Quincy, which had built a branch south from Albia during the early 1880s in

an unsuccessful attempt to thwart an invasion by Gould into Burlington's service area. Failing that, it was soon abandoned, but was eventually, but only partially, used as the Central's short Hocking spur to meet the needs of the Hocking Coal Company, which was formed by Oskaloosa interests on July 7, 1898, for the purpose of buying, selling, and mining coal in Monroe County or elsewhere in Iowa. Initial production reached 600 tons per day but quickly rose to 1,500 tons per day. Indeed, in 1899 Iowa Central boasted that the Hocking Company "operated the largest and most intensive plant in the state of Iowa." The Hocking (inevitably pronounced "Hawkin" by older Central employees) Company itself was acquired by Iowa Central in 1902 and proved to be a profitable source of income for many years.[12]

On another front, on October 23, 1898, Iowa Central had moved its terminal facilities from Keithsburg to Monmouth after the latter community had offered monetary incentives to the company. Subsequently, minor locomotive and car repairs were made at that point, and locomotives and crews were changed there.[13]

Other developments focused on the northern reaches of the road. Since 1886, residents of Algona, the seat of Kossuth County, had looked longingly to the southeast, hoping that the Central's Belmond Branch might be pushed on to their community. A citizens' group had urged the creation of a tax designed to entice the company to build such a line, and the company had, in fact, made a survey. The plan was allowed to slumber for several years, however, before being revived. In the fall of 1898, the various townships voted for a 5 percent tax, and Iowa Central responded by forming the Iowa Central & Western Railroad, chartered under the laws of Iowa on October 27, 1898, to build the line from Belmond to Algona; the townships also donated $50,000 and depot grounds to Iowa Central & Western. This amount plus a large advance from the parent company was sufficient to see the thirty-seven-mile line built to completion by November 1, 1899.[14]

Iowa had been a state since 1846 and was by now essentially settled. Yet there remained manifest opportunities in fledgling towns on the new branch or even in the countryside. Kanawha, said Iowa Central, was "surrounded by the *largest* and *best* agricultural territory of any town in the state" and "had a nucleus of a town for one thousand people." Up the track sixteen miles was St. Benedict, "the center of a wealthy German Catholic community with a $10,000 church . . . and . . . $7,000 Parochial school." St. Benedict was "destined to be a solid, prosperous city" and at the moment had "openings in almost every line of trade." Agricultural opportunities were equally attractive. "Land in Iowa is at last acknowledged to be better than gold mines," gushed George C. Call of Algona, and another real

estate operator claimed that Iowa Central's new branch to that place traversed "the best lands in Iowa." "There are thousands of acres of rich soil in the north and northwestern parts of the state waiting to be developed," chipped in Iowa Central. The E. L. Stilson Land Company at Corwith offered "improved and unimproved farms for sale from 80 acres to 640 acres in a body," and they were "handy to schools, churches, and markets." Iowa Central predictably offered reduced fares for potential immigrants, and H. J. Tremain, owner of The Durall in Algona, urged land prospectors to stay at his fine "new brick hotel" with rates of only $2 per day. "Steam heat in every room," he promised; "twelve rooms with bath, no extra charge for bath on Sunday."[15]

In 1899 and 1900, there was an abundance of rumors that Iowa Central would be expanded elsewhere. One, for instance, was that the Story City Branch would be extended to coalfields in Boone County at Fraser, then on to Callender, and perhaps into South Dakota. Another had the Algona Branch extended to Okoboji, Spirit Lake, and beyond. At Spirit Lake, the *Beacon* assured its readers that Iowa Central would reach that place in 1900. At Estherville, however, the *Vindicator* took exception: "Of course the Iowa Central will build to Estherville," it confidently declared. In fact, the articles of incorporation for Iowa Central & Western did authorize the company to extend the line from Belmond to Algona, and "thence in a northwesterly direction to the northern boundary of the state." Iowa Central & Western likewise had authority to construct a line from Oskaloosa to Des Moines, while earlier maps had shown Central's Newton Branch stretched northwestward through Story City and on to Fort Dodge. But none of it came to pass.[16]

Elsewhere, rumors of a road that would intersect or at least connect with Iowa Central proved true when the Muscatine, North & South Railroad reached Elrick Junction, four miles west of Oakville, in 1899. This twenty-eight-mile pike had

IOWA CENTRAL RAILWAY.

IOWA FARM LANDS

It is a well known fact there are no better farm lands in the world than those in the "Hawkeye State," and the

Iowa Central Railway

traverses the center of this section. There are thousands of acres of rich soil in the north and northwestern parts of the state waiting to be developed. Fine farms can be had at nominal prices.

Iowa's Fine Climate

The climate of Northern and Northwestern Iowa is very healthful. In summer there is no extreme heat, and the evenings are delightfully cool. Reports of the State Board of Health show the death rate to be extremely low, being much less than in many other states.

Cost of Farm Lands

For full information concerning Iowa farm lands, their cost, location, crops, maps and descriptive matter, address any Land Agent whose advertisement appears in this folder, or the

General Passenger and Ticket Agent,

IOWA CENTRAL RAILWAY,

MARSHALLTOWN, IOWA.

Figure 8.12. In 1899, Iowa still held a few undeveloped lands. Iowa Central sought to do its bit in changing this.

IOWA CENTRAL RAILWAY.

FARM LAND IN IOWA

We are the

OLDEST Real Estate Firm in Corwith

We have improved and unimproved farms for sale from 80 acres to 640 acres in a body. These lands are located in Southern Hancock and Kossuth counties. The soil is a black loam, from two to five feet deep with good, clay subsoil,

No Gravel, No Deep Sloughs, No Hills and they are handy to schools, churches and markets.

Write us for Circulars and Maps, which give prices, terms and locations of farms.	If you want a farm in Iowa investigate what we have to offer before you purchase.

To reach Corwith, Iowa, take the IOWA CENTRAL RAILWAY at Peoria, Ill., from all points East, South and Southeast; at Albia, Ia., from all points South, Southeast and Southwest. Corwith is located on the Belmond-Algona division of the IOWA CENTRAL RAILWAY.

E. L. STILSON LAND CO.

CORWITH, IOWA

Figure 8.13. Iowa Central and friends promised marvelously good things along the branch from Hampton through Belmond and Corwith to Algona.

been built south from Muscatine after shippers there had felt abused by the much larger Chicago, Rock Island & Pacific. The Muscatine road eventually took trackage rights over Iowa Central to Oakville and then built on south to Burlington. Fate was unkind, however, and the property bounced back and forth in receivership, but for Iowa Central it was a friendly and useful feeder.[17]

Figure 8.14. During the last years of the nineteenth century, Iowa Central ordered a few locomotives, including 0-6-0 switchers and 2-8-0s for road work. The company's motive power inventory nevertheless remained humble in the extreme, as these photos indicate.

Figure 8.15. Despite its presence at Peoria—which it shared with eleven other roads—Iowa Central always was a home road serving mostly rural and small-town needs. Here American Standard 4-4-0 engine 42, outshopped by Manchester in 1882, was about to wheel the afternoon passenger train out of Peoria to the Hawkeye State. Paul H. Stringham collection.

In 1899, a relatively unknown New Yorker, Robert J. Kimball, was elected to succeed Horace J. Morse as president of the Central. Under President Morse there had been much economizing. His thrifty habits plus a good revenue year had provided a $102,481 surplus and a 3 percent dividend for holders of preferred stock. After paying the dividend, the directors decided to invest in new equipment. They advised the stockholders that orders had been placed for 6 locomotives, 250 coal cars, 250 boxcars, and 25 furniture cars.[18]

Contracts of a different type spelled out changes in the road's operating agreements. By May 1, 1896, the agreement with Burlington, Cedar Rapids & Northern allowing the Central to use trackage between Manly Junction and Northwood had been abrogated by the Sage administration. The previous arrangement had stipulated that a $14,000 annual payment be rendered to Iowa Central for the use of this track, but the new contract allowed both companies to use it, with responsibility for maintenance shared by both the owner and the lessee.[19]

Before the end of the century, yet another contract, short-lived, was signed with the Atchison, Topeka & Santa Fe Railway (AT&SF or Sante Fe), which allowed it to use Iowa Central trackage from Nemo, Illinois, to Monmouth. That agreement facilitated Chicago–Monmouth passenger service by means of Santa Fe from Chicago to Nemo and thence over the Central for the last five miles to Monmouth and Iowa Central's depot. Service was inaugurated on November 5, 1899, but lasted just a short while.[20]

Chapter 9

ENTER THE TWENTIETH CENTURY

When I was young and in my prime,
I went to work for the IC line;
Now I'm old and shot to hell,
And have to work for the M&StL!
—RHYME HEARD OFTEN AROUND THE FORMER IOWA CENTRAL

THE DAWN OF THE TWENTIETH CENTURY came to Iowa Central amid rumors of vast change in corporate ownership. For reasons that are unclear, Russell Sage had relaxed his firm grip on Central stock, and this allowed an eager young man by the name of Edwin Hawley to purchase large blocks of Central securities. Hawley, born in Chatham, New York, in 1850, had started his railroad career as a clerk for the Erie Railroad in June 1867. During his subsequent rise to positions of management, Hawley was associated with several companies and a number of powerful capitalists. Collis P. Huntington, the "California Railroad King," had noticed young Hawley and offered him a position with Southern Pacific (SP). Hawley readily accepted and was associated with SP even after the death of Huntington in 1900. As it developed, Huntington had held a large block of stock in Minneapolis & St. Louis, and in order to look after these financial interests Hawley quietly had been appointed vice president of that company in the autumn of 1894. Hawley was elevated to the presidency of M&StL in October 1896.[1]

When Huntington died, Edward H. Harriman purchased a controlling interest in Southern Pacific, but Hawley retained a position on the board of directors of that road. During this time Hawley attempted to sell M&StL to Harriman, who then controlled Southern Pacific, Union Pacific, and Illinois Central—the latter road connecting with Union Pacific at Council Bluffs and with M&StL at Fort Dodge and Albert Lea.[2]

At this same time M&StL was building its own line from Minneapolis toward Omaha via Winthrop, New Ulm, Estherville, Spencer, and Storm Lake, possibly with the idea of making the road more attractive to Harriman. His purchase of the St. Louis road would have been logical inasmuch as it would have given the Harriman roads a direct Twin Cities conduit. As it developed, however, Hawley did not sell M&StL, the St. Louis road stopped construction on its Omaha line, and Harriman failed to gain a Twin Cities outlet.

Thwarted in his attempt to sell M&StL, Hawley revised his plans; he consolidated his position at M&StL, then proceeded to purchase a controlling interest in Iowa Central. He assumed its presidency in June 1900.[3]

In this way the Iowa company became the corporate brother of Minneapolis & St. Louis. Local

88

Figure 9.1. Edwin Hawley became Iowa Central's president in June 1900.

residents observed, perhaps with a tinge of sadness, that the last remnants of local control had passed with the coming of the new group. Indeed, now all Iowa Central directors were from New York, Chicago, or Minneapolis. There was still much to be thankful for as far as local patrons were concerned, however. The road remained an independent (if weak) competitor, and, they observed, had one of the major east-west roads gained control of Iowa Central, the property might have been raped, plundered, and relegated to the position of a small, insignificant branch-line operation.

The smiles of those with an interest in the Central widened when the new management announced that earnings for fiscal year 1900 were the highest in company history—up 9.68 percent over the previous year. Accordingly, a dividend of 1.5 percent was paid to holders of preferred stock. The

company also announced that it had authorized expenditures for the rebuilding of bridges and other permanent improvements during the coming year.[4]

One of those improvements provided an end-to-end connection with M&StL at Albert Lea. As it developed, the operating and traffic arrangement that Burlington, Cedar Rapids & Northern had had with M&StL for a quarter century dissolved, and the Rock Island–dominated BCR&N built its own line to St. Paul. The Cedar Rapids road, of course, retained trackage rights over Iowa Central from Manly to Northwood, owned its own extension to the state boundary, and leased M&StL's line from that point to Albert Lea. Hawley now had Iowa Central run over its own property from Mason City to Northwood and then on to Albert Lea by rights over BCR&N and M&StL to share a common yard with M&StL.[5]

Soon thereafter, Hawley issued a spate of announcements having to do with changes and improvements. For example, Iowa Central took a fifty-year lease on the Iowa Central & Western (the Belmond–Algona Branch). It was merely a formality, of course, since the parent company had operated the line since its inception. At the same time, the new management announced that it had issued and sold $2 million in bonds to buy the Keithsburg Bridge Company; the deed of sale was conveyed to Iowa Central on July 23, 1901. In addition, the Hawley group, complaining bitterly about previous managers who supposedly had left the property "in a mess," ordered the road renovated. Orders went out to rebuild bridges and reduce all grades to a maximum of less than 1 percent. Hawley was true to his word. In 1902 and 1903, for example, crews reduced grades and curvature between Searsboro and Oak Grove, where trainmen constantly had complained that the original alignment was "crooked as a billy goat's tail." To facilitate this and other projects of a similar nature, Hawley ordered fifty ballast cars. And in an effort to move a rising volume of business, he placed orders for

Figure 9.2. The Keithsburg Bridge Company was conveyed to Iowa Central on July 23, 1901.

750 boxcars, 100 gondolas, 150 stockcars, and 12 locomotives. The road also acquired the old Central Hotel across the street to the northwest from the passenger station at Oskaloosa and remodeled it into a freight depot and office building.[6]

Other news was mixed. Revenues were down in 1901, while expenses were up; there would be only a small surplus. And, to gain efficiencies, much of the force from Iowa Central's Marshalltown headquarters was transferred to Minneapolis and dovetailed with that of M&StL. Prospects seemed bleak. The years 1903 and 1904 were notable for

the recessions that gripped the Iowa Central service area as well as much of the country. In 1903 Iowa also was blighted by excessive rains and by an early frost, which curtailed normally heavy agricultural production. The following year produced conditions that were no better. Matters changed by degree. Word came in the late summer of 1905 that the Central's revenues were up by almost 10 percent, but operating expenses practically negated any gain: there was no surplus. Nevertheless, much ballasting, bridge renovation, and grade reduction was accomplished during the year. But Hawley rejected requests for heavier motive power, and Iowa Central's inventory remained modest in the extreme, with American Standard 4-4-0s predominating, supplemented by larger locomotives in the form of six Moguls (2-6-0s) and twenty-six Ten Wheelers (4-6-0s), all in freight service.[7]

Iowa Central's modest American Standard 4-4-0s would be assigned to the *North Star Limited,* launched in November 1902 for the

Figure 9.3. The crew of Work Extra 105 was assigned to gangs easing grades and curvature. Vaughn R. Ward collection.

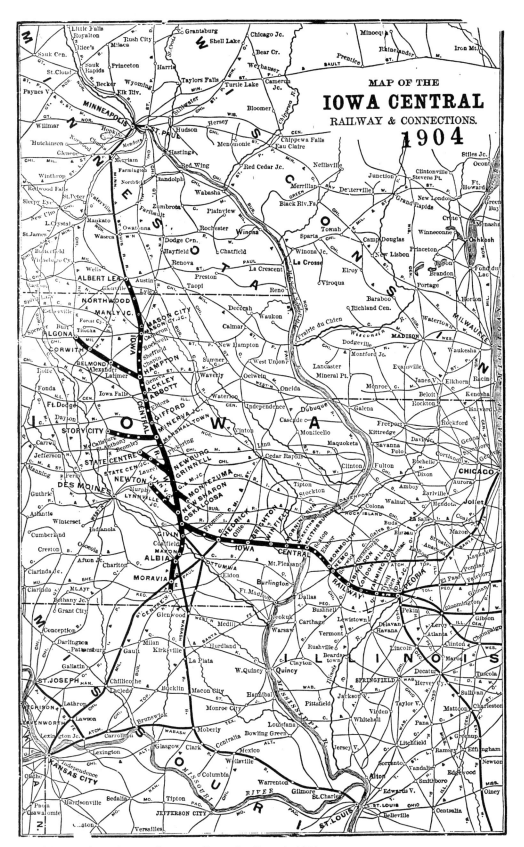

Map 9.1. Iowa Central was at the apex of its track mileage in 1904.

Figure 9.4. New power came to supplement relatively new locomotives, such as ten-wheeler 108 (Pittsburgh, 1897), but Iowa Central's stable of power remained humble in the extreme.

Minneapolis–St. Louis trade by Minneapolis & St. Louis (Minneapolis–Albert Lea) in conjunction with Iowa Central (Albert Lea–Albia) and Wabash (Albia–St. Louis). Anson B. Cutts, responsible for passenger matters at both M&StL and Iowa Central, lost no opportunity to promote the *North Star* in every season—especially, in 1904, as a princely way for patrons to reach the fabulous Louisiana Purchase Exposition at St. Louis. Cutts pointed out that travelers on the *North Star* could get a "full view of the grounds and buildings" from the cars. He was right. Of all St. Louis railroads, Wabash was most actively engaged in the fair; its line was adjacent to the grounds, and it built a special if temporary station just outside the gates. When the extravaganza opened, Wabash ran a fleet of trains to and from Union Station downtown and, in the end, handled more fair passengers than

any other single road. Iowa Central joined M&StL in offering attractive round-trip fares; the cars thronged with persons anxious to see a plethora of agricultural wonders in the "Iowa Building" as well as any number of additional wonderful sights.[8]

Elsewhere, on January 16, 1905, traffic arrangements were made with Chicago, Burlington & Quincy to handle freight between Oskaloosa and Des Moines at an agreed rate per loaded car. This agreement allowed a connection of sorts between the southern portions of Iowa Central and M&StL at Des Moines.[9]

Iowa Central enjoyed a good year in 1906, earning a surplus. Transportation revenues were up 14.31 percent over the previous year, while operating expenses were up only 2.85 percent. At the same time, the road was replacing ancient iron rails with steel, and lighter steel rails with heavier steel, thus "manifesting the wisdom of the present management in making expenditures to bring the property to . . . a high standard of efficiency" in the words of the road's annual report.[10]

Opportunities to showcase Iowa Central were few, and clearly its track structure and equipment suffered by comparison with those of the giant roads that surrounded it. The track from Manly to Albert Lea, owned variously, was heavily trafficked by Rock Island and Iowa Central (also by Illinois Central from Glenville to Albert Lea) and was necessarily well maintained, and on that stretch Iowa Central crews were able to "show their stuff" in moving trains. But there really was no "racetrack" part of the railroad—not officially, at least. East of Marshalltown, however, Iowa Central paralleled Chicago & North Western for a few miles, and enginemen of both roads frequently succumbed to ego impulses and racing fever. For example, one C&NW engineer recalled heading west with a passenger train just as an Iowa Central passenger from Oskaloosa appeared; the race was on. "The Central passenger trains are pulled by Hinkley engines with a valve motion that takes one's breath away," the C&NW man said admiringly. "The Hinkley was sending rockets fifty feet from the top of her stack, and the big wheels of the saucy little jade were turning like electric fans. . . . Smoke from the stack of that Central engine was trailing back in a straight line." Fortunately, both trains stopped without incident at Marshalltown's joint station; the platform conversation among passengers and crewmen, sad to say, went unrecorded.[11]

Russell Sage died on July 22, 1906. Sage had been associated with the road practically from its inception; he had served as director, vice president, and president. His habits, monetary and otherwise, had become legendary in Iowa and across the entire country. He had been accused, among other things, of being somber, crafty, and reclusive. W. B. Davids, a Hawley lieutenant in New York, called

Sage "the meanest man who ever lived." His years as president of the Central certainly had been noted for "economies," as he had not characteristically plowed money back into the property. On the other hand, Sage did not plunder the road, as he was said to have done with other companies. As a matter of fact, he seems to have had an affection for the Iowa road, although it was certainly never one of his great moneymakers.[12]

No communities took more interest in Iowa Central than Oskaloosa and Marshalltown—each a crew-change point, each with company repair facilities, each with a sizable number of railway employees as residents, and each with an appreciable customer base. In addition to the usual assortment of merchant tailors, milliners, grocers, and professional offices, Oskaloosa boasted no fewer than ten cigar makers, eight hotels, five lumberyards, five carriage and wagon builders, four boiler manufacturers, four harness makers, three foundries, two flour mills, two garment manufacturers, two broom factories, and one wholesale grocer.[13]

Marshalltown, proud headquarters city for the company, had been disappointed when the general offices were moved to Minneapolis. Yet Marshalltown still boasted the Central's general shops and terminal facilities. In 1907 there were 564 men and boys employed at the shops earning an annual combined salary of $360,000: the shops, easily the largest single employer in town, supported "every ninth man, woman and child in the city." Marshalltown was, indeed, proud of both Iowa Central and the employees of the company. *Marshalltown Illustrated* put it this way: "Its men mostly are a highly skilled class of worker, commanding high wages, owning good homes, and constituting an exceptionally desirable class of citizens because of their intelligence, their plane of living and their purchasing power."[14]

Marshalltown clearly was an important place on the Iowa Central. An average of sixty-six locomotives were overhauled annually in the machine shop, the rolling stock of the company was maintained by the car and paint shops, the twenty-two-stall roundhouse handled the routine servicing of motive power, extra gangs and bridge and building gangs were headquartered there, trains were switched and made up in its yard, the stores department serviced the entire system from that location, and less-than-carload shipments were handled by a large force there.[15]

If Marshalltown professed pride in Iowa Central, the favor was not always returned by the company's senior management. Just before Edwin Hawley arrived on the scene, the road's on-site management (i.e., the general manager, who was stationed at Marshalltown) carefully plotted a move of the road's headquarters to Peoria, Iowa Central's "principal gateway," where "affiliated connecting lines" could be cultivated. However, beneath that plan,

which was worthy from a strategic standpoint, lay the truth: in March 1900 general manager T. E. Clarke seethed at favors that Marshalltown had apparently granted upstart and bit player Chicago Great Western, which merely passed through town, unlike Iowa Central, which had a profound presence; according to Clarke, Iowa Central paid out "in cash," some "forty thousand dollars per month on average," while its local earnings "did not exceed seven thousand dollars." In a confidential letter to BCR&N's C. J. Ives, Clarke charged that from Marshalltown there had been "no tangible evidence of any appreciation for same." It was, he said, "impossible for this company to secure the loyal services of a local attorney to represent us against any kind of unfair treatment," and "our official and personal actions are the constant subject of gossip on the streets and other public places." But it had gotten out that Iowa Central's headquarters

Figure 9.5. Marshalltown was the base for Iowa Central's wrecker and crew, which saw frequent activity. Here men and equipment were picking up the wreckage from a nasty accident at Manly on November 5, 1909.

Figure 9.6. The Marshalltown-based relief train paused at the Gifford water tank in 1910.

might be moved to Peoria, and this had resulted in no fewer than 782 letters of complaint from up and down the line against removal of the general offices. In Marshalltown, fumed Clarke, the cry against removal came not from shippers but from vested interests—real estate owners, shopkeepers, doctors, barbers, blacksmiths, and others who stood to lose if Iowa Central shifted many employees elsewhere. He, and he alone, had final authority as to the move, said Clarke, giving every clue that his bags were packed for Peoria. But when Hawley appeared, the move made was to Minneapolis, and Clarke was not invited.[16]

The panic of 1907, new Iowa and Illinois laws reducing passenger and freight rates, and the loss of the Marshalltown car and paint shops by fire on October 25, 1907, combined to drop the Central's operating revenue in fiscal year 1908 by over 4 percent. Fortunately, though, the road had an adequate surplus, and although the board of directors declined to pay any dividends, it did continue

to install eighty-pound steel rail on the main line. Moreover, Hawley was pleased to announce that new industries had been attracted:

Northwestern Portland Cement, Mason City
American Brick and Tile, Mason City
Sheffield Brick and Tile, Sheffield
Albia Coal Company, Albia
National Coal Company, Middle Grove,
     Illinois

Other customers were mundane in nature but in the aggregate produced significant traffic. These included but were not restricted to creameries at Latimer and Liscomb, wagon makers at Ewart and Wayland, wholesale grocers at Marshalltown and Peoria, overalls manufacturers at Abingdon and Oskaloosa, ice shippers at Kensett and Grinnell, meatpackers at Albia and Mason City, potato shippers at Algona and Geneva, and makers of clay products at Corwith and Little York. Agricultural implements were billed at Monmouth, washing machines at Newton, canned vegetables at Gilman, and pickles at Oakville. Lumberyards, coal dealers, and grain elevators were ubiquitous. Horses were shipped at Albia, Grinnell, Little York, London Mills, Morning Sun, and New Sharon, among other places. Cattle and hogs flowed from nearly every station. Taintor, on the Newton Branch, was a busy shipping point, as were Wayland and Winfield, on the main line.[17]

Increased traffic volumes required additions to the company's car fleet, Hawley reported. By mid-1908, Iowa Central owned forty-five pieces of passenger equipment (including the office car *Hawkeye*), as well as 2,924 freight cars (of which 1,746 were boxcars and 836 were coal/flatcars). Most of the coal/flatcars were assigned to the many mines that the Iowa Central served. Load sizes from these important customers had increased, and the

company had been obliged to acquire larger cars and heavier locomotives. This caused problems, however.[18]

The Mississippi River bridge at Keithsburg had weight restrictions that demanded tonnage reductions on both sides of the river. Thus, for example, a train from Oskaloosa would have to reduce its tonnage at Elrick, requiring a second train from Elrick to Keithsburg, where the original tonnage had to be "doubled together" on the first train before it could proceed to Monmouth. This expensive and time-consuming operation had become intolerable (see Table 9.1 for increases in tonnage crossing the Mississippi), and in order to solve the problem, Iowa Central petitioned Congress, asking that it be allowed to build a new span sixty feet upstream from the old bridge. Permission came on February 13, 1909, and the railroad quickly awarded a construction contract to the McClintock-Marshall

Figure 9.7. Hawley authorized acquisition of new power, such as Mogul 200, ordered from Baldwin in 1908, but Iowa Central never boasted heavy and advanced locomotive technology.

Figure 9.8. Iowa Central's inventory of rolling stock rarely matched customer demand.

Company of Pittsburgh. The handsome new structure was designed with a 233-foot lift span; it was placed in service during 1910.[19]

Table 9.1. Tonnage crossing the Mississippi, 1885–1908

Year	Eastbound tonnage	Westbound tonnage	Total
1885	45,375	23,175	68,550
1890	164,911	90,447	355,355
1895	113,573	138,053	251,626
1900	467,509	355,243	822,752
1905	397,379	609,117	1,006,506
1908	333,151	846,545	1,179,686

Source: Iowa Board of Railroad Commissioners Reports *for 1885, 1890, 1895, 1900, 1905, and 1908.*

The cash requirements for the new bridge at Keithsburg and the company's financial performance in 1909 mirrored what had become Iowa Central's constant dilemma. The road had a net deficit that year, but by selling obsolete rolling stock for scrap and by issuing equipment notes and certificates, Hawley was able to take delivery of 20 new locomotives and 692 freight cars. There was no choice, Hawley argued, if the road was to be competitive. But net income from operations was historically thin, and these massive expenditures were sure to put pressure on Iowa Central's ability to service debt. Again, said Hawley, there was no choice.[20]

Iowa Central had been an important coal carrier since the inception of its earliest predecessor. Indeed, one of the basic reasons for building the road had been to supply the country to the west and north with coal from central and southern Iowa. The coal beds in Hardin County had not proved to be as abundant as had been originally thought, but deposits in Appanoose, Monroe, and Mahaska Counties were found to be as large, if not larger,

Figure 9.9. Work began on the bridge approaches in 1909.

Figure 9.10. "Bridge monkeys" came from near and far to work on Iowa Central's impressive bridge at Keithsburg.

Figure 9.11. Progress on the new bridge was most agreeable in 1909. The old structure can be seen to the right.

Figure 9.12. The lengthy approach from the east eventually would be filled in.

Figure 9.13. In 1909, Iowa Central replaced the swing span bridge over the Mississippi with a lift span. The steamboat *Black Hawk* passed southbound while workmen on the new structure took a break.

Figure 9.14. A southbound steamer passed under the new lift span and through the open swing span of the old bridge.

than had been estimated. Entire trains moved routinely from mines along the Iowa Central to destinations far removed. Chicago, Milwaukee & St. Paul, for instance, received regular shipments at Capron (on the State Center Branch) for use as locomotive fuel. Other railroads also purchased large quantities of coal for fuel, and of course southern Iowa mines supplied the everyday needs of both industry and the public.[21]

Throughout the 1890s and into the new century, coal—"wonderful carboniferous treasurers" as one early writer put it—remained the crown jewel of the Central's traffic mix, ranging from 43.4 percent of all its tonnage in 1892 to 70.7 percent in

1898. In terms of coal handled by all railroads in Iowa, the company moved 12.4 percent in 1890 and 22.6 percent in 1899, averaging 20.2 percent for the decade. These were salient numbers, because coal mining ranked behind only agriculture as the state's major industry from 1880 to 1930. Mahaska County, with mines at Muchakinock, Excelsior, and other locations around Oskaloosa, was the state leader until 1901, when it was superseded by Monroe County, with bountiful coal beds at Hocking and elsewhere in the Albia area.[22]

During the first ten years of the twentieth century, Iowa Central handled an average of 847,000 tons of soft coal per year—which represented growth

Figure 9.15. The superior quality of Iowa Central's new bridge at Keithsburg (top) and the lengthy open-deck steel trestle on the Iowa approach (bottom) seemed curiously out of character for the road.

of nearly 100 percent over the 1880s and about 50 percent over the 1890s. Much of this increase derived from new mines in Monroe County (Albia Coal Company, for instance, came onto the scene in 1908), but much was billed from recently opened pits along the line in Illinois. National Coal Mining Company, which commenced operation at Middle Grove in 1908, was only one of many producers that Iowa Central served on the Peoria line. Back in Iowa, the Hook & Eye continued to handle about one-fifth of all coal moved by rail, ranking behind Rock Island and North Western most years, but second only to Rock Island in 1905 and 1910.[23]

"Miners' trains" were regularly run to coal camps at Maxwell, Farmington, and Hocking. Iowa Central owned eight miners' cars (boxcars with benches), and a typical arrangement, for example, saw a train crew on hand at Albia at 6:00 a.m., ready to take workers to the mines at Hocking. After depositing the men at their work station, the train crew went back to Albia, ate breakfast, and returned with a "cut" of empty cars for the mines. Empties were "spotted" for loading, and then cars of loaded coal were gathered up and taken to Albia. This process continued all during the day until the miners' shift ended at 6:00 p.m. It was grounds for dismissal to delay the miners' train in either direction, and these trains moved with express train precision. After the miners had been returned to Albia, the train crew went back to the mines with empty cars and picked up the last loads of the day. Upon delivery of these cars to the Albia yard, the "mine run" could "tie up."[24]

Not only was Iowa Central a coal-oriented railroad, it also had substantial interest in various mining operations—investments totaling $619,710.56 in 1911. To be sure, it had fully purchased the Hocking Coal Company in 1902.[25]

One way that a railroad is judged is by the quality of its track structure. Frankly, Iowa Central was never accused of having an astonishingly

smooth roadbed. The main line was fairly well ballasted with gravel during the Hawley years, but as late as 1910 more than 40 percent of its mileage was ballasted merely with soil, cinders, or slack. The original iron rails had been replaced on all but short stretches of certain branch lines; eighty-pound (to the yard) steel rails had been laid to most of the main line. Several grades had been reduced, and the track had been relocated in a few instances; work to lower the grade northbound out of the Skunk River bottoms from Oskaloosa to Lacey was especially noteworthy. Tie plates were applied on curves between Mason City and Marshalltown, and in the years 1909–11 Iowa Central undertook a serious campaign to strengthen bridges, modernize and standardize signage, improve grade, build or upgrade right-of-way fences, and generally enhance the property. Still, the usual policy was to "economize" first in the area of track maintenance. Therefore, when the company experienced any downturn in revenues, a number of track workers were laid off; maintenance of way slipped accordingly until prosperity returned.[26]

As Iowa Central grew in mileage and in volume of traffic, employment on the road rose correspondingly. Table 9.2 indicates such growth from 1878 through 1911. Whenever it could, Iowa Central hired locally. In 1906 trainmaster J. H. McCarthy wired all Iowa Central station agents: "It is the purpose of this company between now and fall to place a number of young men on the road as students . . . to learn the duties of brakemen and to be employed in that capacity when they have become familiar with the work." He continued: "If you are acquainted with any young men at your station who desire to enter this service, I wish you would have them make application to me, but endorsed by you." Specifically, McCarthy was looking for "young men between the ages of 21 and 26 years, weighing from 125# to 160#, of steady habits, and fair education."[27]

STEAM SHOVEL
GIFFORD, IA.

Figure 9.16. Iowa Central took trainloads of ballast out of gravel pits near Gifford. Vaughn R. Ward collection.

Table 9.2. Numbers of Iowa Central employees, 1878–1911

Year	Number of employees	Year	Number of employees
1878	514	1895	1,031
1880	600	1900	1,091
1885	1,100	1905	2,584
1890	1,131	1911	2,017

Source: Iowa Board of Railroad Commissioners Reports *for 1878, 1880, 1885, 1890, 1895, 1900, 1905, and 1911.*

But Iowa Central was notorious for paying low wages. Records show that daily average compensation was $1.93 in 1893, $1.82 in 1898, and $2.37 in 1911. In 1893, road engineers received from $2.75 per day for switch engine service to $3.70 "per hundred miles" for preferred runs. By 1903, engineers were drawing up to $4.10 per hundred miles if assigned to the company's heaviest freight locomotives; passenger engineers were allowed $3.50 per hundred miles. Firemen were paid on a percentage basis, in 1893 amounting to 58 percent of an engineer's wage for the same mileage on the same type of locomotive. By 1907, passenger conductors on preferred runs were drawing $130 a month, while brakemen were earning $60 a month for assignment on the same trains. It was hard work and low wages for employees even after the union movement belatedly reached Iowa Central.[28]

Not surprisingly, the road frequently suffered labor problems. The Hawley management, typical

Figure 9.17. The crew called for this passenger run seemed well pleased with the patriotic decking on locomotive 16—an elderly 4-4-0 acquired by Central Railroad of Iowa back in 1871. It was unlikely that any member of the crew had been in service that long; Iowa Central and its predecessor were always "boomer roads," where employees came and went as if through a turnstile. Vaughn R. Ward collection.

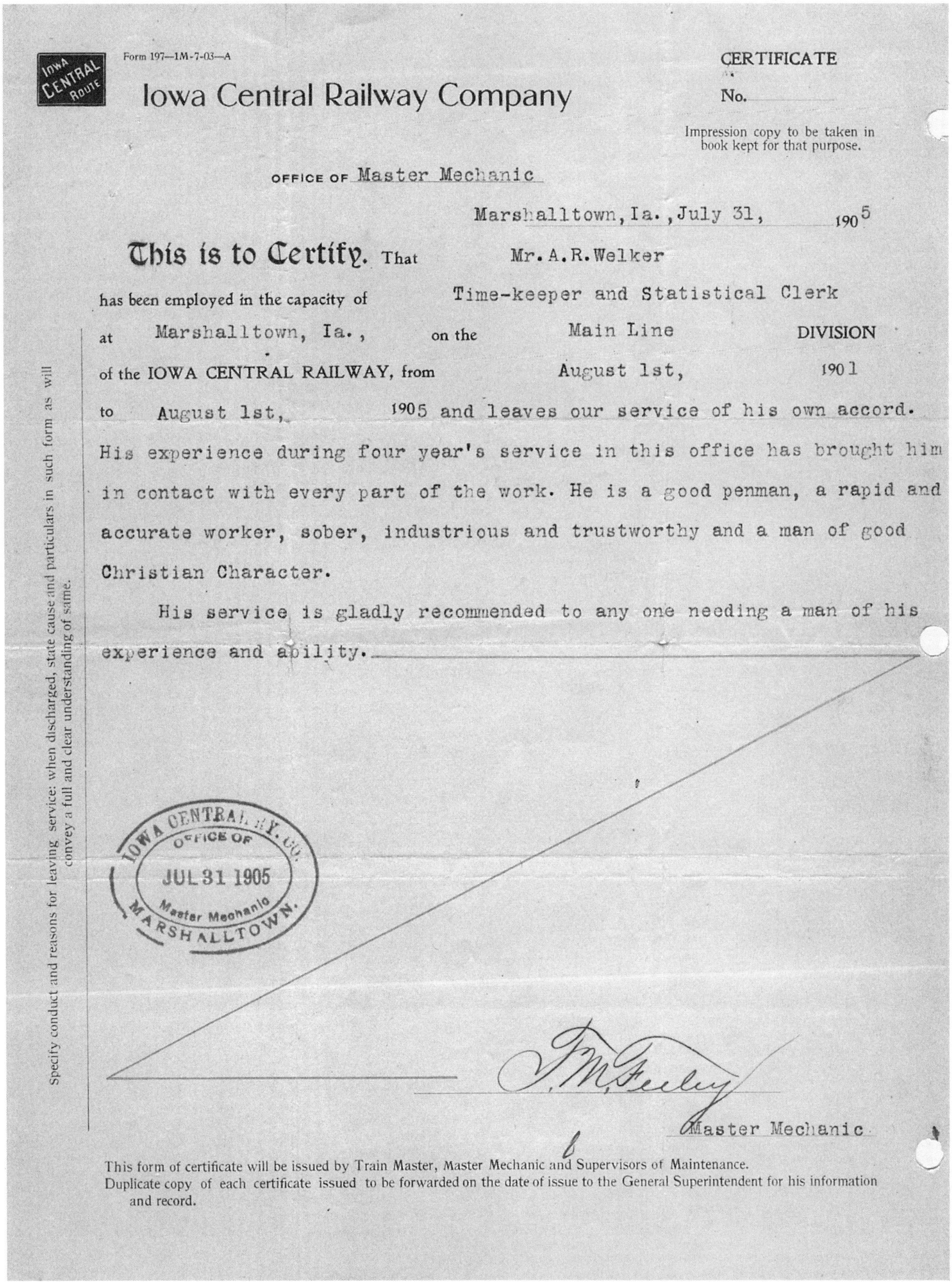

Form 197—1M-7-03—A

IOWA CENTRAL ROUTE

Iowa Central Railway Company

CERTIFICATE

No.

Impression copy to be taken in book kept for that purpose.

OFFICE OF Master Mechanic

Marshalltown, Ia., July 31, 1905

This is to Certify. That Mr. A. R. Welker

has been employed in the capacity of Time-keeper and Statistical Clerk

at Marshalltown, Ia., on the Main Line DIVISION

of the IOWA CENTRAL RAILWAY, from August 1st, 1901

to August 1st, 1905 and leaves our service of his own accord. His experience during four year's service in this office has brought him in contact with every part of the work. He is a good penman, a rapid and accurate worker, sober, industrious and trustworthy and a man of good Christian Character.

His service is gladly recommended to any one needing a man of his experience and ability.

IOWA CENTRAL RY. CO. OFFICE OF JUL 31 1905 Master Mechanic MARSHALLTOWN.

F. M. Feeley

Master Mechanic

Specify conduct and reasons for leaving service; when discharged, state cause and particulars in such form as will convey a full and clear understanding of same.

This form of certificate will be issued by Train Master, Master Mechanic and Supervisors of Maintenance.
Duplicate copy of each certificate issued to be forwarded on the date of issue to the General Superintendent for his information and record.

Figure 9.18. Employees came and went with great regularity.

Figure 9.19. Trainmaster McCarthy was looking for "young men between the ages of 21 and 26 years, weighing from 125# to 160#, of steady habits, and fair education."

Figure 9.20. Despite long hours, hard work, and poor pay, local boys found engine service irresistible. One of these was Merle Mahaffey, in the gangway, who hired out as an Iowa Central fireman on June 3, 1904, and retired as a senior locomotive engineer for M&StL in October 1960.

of those at the time, fully resisted unionization. For years Iowa Central had been a "boomer" railroad where one could get a job at the drop of a hat—and leave just as quickly—but this tradition was coming to an end during the early years of the twentieth century, as railroad employees sought rights under the banner of brotherhoods. A number of benefits were won for Central train crews in 1907, but when machinists, boilermakers, blacksmiths, and helpers went on strike in 1908, they were replaced with non-union laborers. "It was very bad," said M&StL's Anson B. Cutts in recalling the strike. Edwin Hawley had little sympathy with the strikers, but he privately reprimanded L. F. Day and other managers for their conduct during those try-

ing days. In any event, the strike and the resultant defeat for organized labor dealt a severe blow to the union movement. Financial losses of employees were somewhat recouped in 1909 and 1910, however, when management grudgingly granted wage increases. President Hawley complained to the stockholders about these increased costs, noting that "while many wage increases have been granted, the labor problem still confronts your management."[29]

Edwin Hawley resigned as president of Iowa Central in 1910, but retained the powerful position of board chairman. Hawley was succeeded as president by T. P. Shonts, who was no stranger to the road, for he had grown up in Iowa's Appanoose

Figure 9.21. Iowa Central was able to recruit a surprising pool of talent, including Samuel F. B. Morse, left, who hired out as a telegrapher at Hampton, where this photo was taken in 1911, and retired as a respected agent at Middle Grove more than fifty years later.

Figure 9.22. This engine crew obligingly posed 4-4-0 engine 28 on the Milwaukee diamond (crossing) at Hedrick, and an unknown photographer playfully wrote in "Solid ORT" (Order of Railroad Telegraphers) as if it were part of legitimate company stenciling on the tender. The plug for ORT likely repeats what cannot be read on the sign held by one of the men on the tender's toolbox. Vaughn R. Ward collection.

County near Centerville, graduated from Monmouth College at Monmouth, and even helped build a portion of the company's Peoria extension.[30]

Shonts announced that Iowa Central had attained a new record for net operating revenue in 1910, but he hastened to add that the road still had a sizable deficit. In fact, Shonts was clearly unhappy about Iowa Central's financial circumstances. He pointed out, for instance, that there had been a 33.49 percent increase in operating expenses over the previous year. In this regard, he complained bitterly about new federal regulations designed to limit the number of continuous hours that train crews and dispatchers were allowed to work. He further groused that state laws had fixed passenger rates at a mere 2 cents per traveled mile. Despite low

net operating revenues, however, Shonts promised to pursue a policy designed to upgrade the road's plant, boasting that 129,075 new cross ties had been installed during 1910.[31]

At the same time, though, Marshalltown shop forces noticed that pieces of Iowa Central rolling stock were missing. They further observed that certain equipment was being removed from along the line. Similarly, the storekeeper observed that he had a very short inventory of essential supplies and replacement items. It soon was evident to them that Edwin Hawley was attempting to realize some "grand design." Indeed, by now Hawley controlled M&StL as well as Iowa Central; Toledo, St. Louis & Western Railroad; and Chicago & Alton, and it was Hawley's dream to unify control of these four companies, thereby consolidating equipment, supplies, shopping facilities, and even general offices. The corporate headquarters was in fact moved to Chicago for a time, although a true consolidation was never accomplished. During this same time, rumors also circulated to the effect that Hawley was attempting to develop some type of transcontinental system, and newspaper editors along the Iowa Central wondered openly what role the local road might play in such a design.[32]

Transcontinental notions notwithstanding, the Hawley empire suffered a modest defeat in south-

ern Iowa during the late fall of 1910. Russell Sage had been the dominant figure in the affairs of the Albia & Centerville Railway, and of course that road had been leased to Iowa Central, which then operated its trains to the Appanoose County seat of Centerville. Following the death of Sage, in the subsequent settlement of his estate, the Sage interests were sold on January 21, 1910, to W. A. Noland, a prominent "interurban man" who, by virtue of his controlling interest in the Centerville road, reorganized the company into the Southern Iowa Traction Company on February 9, 1910. Iowa

Figure 9.23. Iowa Central celebrated record revenues in 1910. The scene at Steamboat Rock implied such good news—a passenger train on the main, a freight passing through the house track, and the elevator track cluttered with cars. It was an image typical during the age of railways.

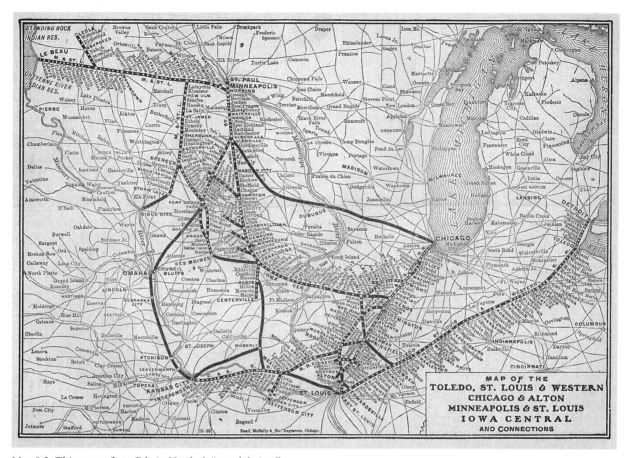

Map 9.2. This map reflects Edwin Hawley's "grand design."

Central's management had been little concerned about these developments because the Centerville enterprise was still under lease to the Central. Moreover, it owed the lessee a considerable amount of money. Nevertheless, the new owners of the Southern Iowa Traction Company were intent upon assuming control of their property. To that end they "secretly decided to take the road by force." One participant in the takeover remembered it as follows:

> November 26, 1910, at 8:00 a.m. was the date and hour we were to go over the top. We borrowed a coach, engine, train and engine crew from the C.B.&Q. here [at Centerville] and followed the regular M&StL [sic] train out of here (after fixing the telegraph wire so it would not work) without their [Iowa Central's] knowledge, without a train order or any rights whatever and arrived at Albia in due time after stopping wherever we found an employee discharging him as an A.&C. employee and hiring him as an employee of the S.I.T. Company. The M&StL [sic] in some way heard we were coming and arranged that we would be allowed to go to their depot and then block the track so we could not get out and in that way compel us to sue for peace, but we anticipated this and staid [sic] on our own rails at Albia during the several days it took to fix matters up.

Iowa Central took the matter to the courts, but eventually lost the option of running its trains into Centerville. Thus a colorful chapter in the history of the Hook & Eye came to an end.[33]

Figure 9.24. Iowa Central suffered a defeat, losing leased trackage between Albia and Centerville that became the Southern Iowa Traction Company. The freight motor with the train seen here is on the Albia line.

Figure 9.25. Southern Iowa erected a carbarn at Centerville to protect and maintain its fleet of electrified equipment.

Fiscal 1911 closed with Iowa Central showing a net deficit of over $16,000. Nevertheless, gross operating revenues were up almost 4.5 percent over 1910. At the same time, Shonts had continued to improve the property by laying thirty-one miles of eighty-pound rail, renovating six depots, and purchasing ten new "heavy" (2-8-0) freight locomotives from Baldwin Locomotive Works at a total cost of $179,837.07. Shonts also was obliged to allocate scarce resources to construction of a new roundhouse at Marshalltown after the old one burned. Shonts was especially proud of the "extra large" sixty-five-foot turntable installed as a part of the new locomotive facility.[34]

Newman F. Erb replaced T. P. Shonts as president on July 1, 1911. Erb was trained as a lawyer and had become involved in the railroad industry shortly after his graduation from law school. He obviously was a "Hawley man" and was elected to the presidency of M&StL at the same time that he

took the helm of Iowa Central. M&StL and the Central, of course, had been affectionate and corporate brothers for a number of years, and it was not surprising to see the president of M&StL hold the same office with Iowa Central.[35]

Shonts and Erb uniformly supported campaigns to boost Iowa Central's competitive position. When M&StL and BCR&N had fallen out of company at the turn of the century, M&StL's Chicago traffic had been shunted over to Illinois Central at Albert Lea, while its St. Louis business was routed over Iowa Central and Wabash. Soon thereafter the ambitious Anson B. Cutts, general passenger and ticket agent for both M&StL and Iowa Central, sought to drum up business for new Minneapolis–Chicago and Minneapolis–St. Louis trains. Indeed, at the suggestion of Cutts, the affected roads agreed to sponsor the *North Star Limited*. This flyer featured "Through Vestibuled, Gas-Lighted Pullman Buffet Sleepers, Chair Cars and First-Class Coaches between

Figure 9.26. Consolidation engine 421 was nearly new when it suffered this embarrassing incident at Steamboat Rock on April 26, 1911.

St. Paul, Minneapolis, and St. Louis . . . Dining Car between Albia and St. Louis."[36]

Iowa Central also offered "Weekly Tourist Car Service" between Los Angeles and St. Paul in conjunction with Santa Fe, Wabash, and M&StL. Under this plan a passenger could board a tourist sleeper in Los Angeles on a Tuesday evening and arrive in St. Paul the following Saturday morning. Also popular for many years were "Homeseekers Excursions." Agents sold tickets for these excursions at "one fare plus two dollars . . . on [the] first and third Tuesdays of each month to points in Oregon, Washington, Utah, Montana, Nebraska, etc.," and on every Tuesday to points in Iowa, Minnesota, South Dakota, Manitoba, and the Canadian Northwest. These were not without success. An eighteen-car emigrant train including two coaches bearing fifty to sixty persons heading for Breckenridge, Minnesota, rolled off the Story City Branch late in March 1902, for example, and on February 24, 1910, R. F. Hale of Winfield plunked down $40 at the ticket window and bought passage for his "Emigrant outfit including four horses" in one boxcar to Leola, South Dakota, via Albert Lea and M&StL. In a similar vein, a few days earlier Iowa Central had rushed a boxcar to Clemon's Grove on the Story City Branch "to load emigrants to Lebanon, Missouri."[37]

Iowa Central's primary enthusiasm for passenger business, however, was quite predictably vested in its regularly scheduled main line trains. In addition to the *North Star Limited,* Iowa Central also sported the *St. Louis and Kansas City Mail,* a day train that ran to and from Albia, connecting there with Wabash. Also serving main line stations was the daily-except-Sunday *Peoria Mail,* which operated between Mason City and Peoria. If one was not satisfied with these offerings, one could almost always purchase transportation aboard the many local freight trains. Patrons were notified, however, that they would be expected to ride in the

Figure 9.27 A. B. Cutts was delighted to sell the road's *North Star Limited* as a premier train.

caboose—and that "no checked baggage" would be handled aboard those trains.

Taking passage on Iowa Central's cabooses and coaches seemed rather more appropriate, however, than "dusting the cushions" on "High Back Chair Cars" assigned to "varnish" trains such as the *North*

Figure 9.28. The celebrated and jointly sponsored *North Star Limited* passed through Iowa during hours of darkness to afford morning arrivals in both St. Louis and Minneapolis/St. Paul.

Star Limited. Likewise, way stations like Chapin and Seaton seemed more appropriate to Iowa Central than Peoria's Union Depot or even facilities at Albert Lea, Marshalltown, and Grinnell, which the company shared with M&StL, C&NW, and Rock

Island, respectively. Iowa Central, after all, was a peculiarly Iowan institution—the Peoria appendage notwithstanding. It was unceremonious and unglamorous, but functional; despite its mostly dreary financial record, it was remarkably spunky. These were values deeply embedded in the character of the Hawkeye State; small wonder that Iowans were protective of the Hook & Eye, even as they poked fun at it. In an emotional sense it was *their* railroad. The Central was the means by which shoppers could get from Lacey to Oskaloosa on the morning train, returning by the up train later in the day; it was the same from Dillon to Marshalltown, especially on Saturdays. Iowa Central provided transport for the first bride who ever left Fremont on a honeymoon; it brought a special Pullman exhibit car from New York to demonstrate "X-ray—the marvel of the ages" to country folk at stations west of Hedrick; it delivered the future honorary secretary of the American Friends Service Committee to William Penn College at Oskaloosa and then took him to court his future wife at Union; it delivered students to the Methodist-sponsored Albion Seminary; it took a couple from St. Anthony to Marshalltown to be married, and a man from the same community to Clemons to work in a grocery store; it delivered throngs of patrons to the Marshall County Fair; it provided an excursion from Corwith for baseball fans to see Algona play Sioux City, and another special train to State Center for the "Grand Reunion and Parade" of the Odd Fellows; it handled aging members of the Grand Army of the Republic from Peoria and Monmouth to encampment at Minneapolis, and the Mahara Minstrels

Lodge from an engagement at Winfield to the Muscatine, North & South at Elrick Junction; it brought mail and express to Abingdon, Abbott, and Ackley, and also to Marietta, Moningers, and Minerva; and, at Albion and all of the Albion-like communities on the system, it provided daily opportunities for locals to stroll to the depot at "train time" to "meet the train," to watch its arrival, to view the hubub, to see who got on and who got off, to see the train's departure—indeed, to perfect one of the great social institutions in rural America during the age of the railways.[38]

Passenger operations were admittedly eye-catching, but freight, as always, remained the apple of Iowa Central's eye. After Hawley gained control of the road, he ordered an important unified freight traffic pattern whereby shipments moved over the joint M&StL–Iowa Central route to and from Peoria. And to facilitate swift handling of through traffic between Minneapolis and Peoria, M&StL and Iowa Central together instituted four "time freight" runs—trains 94, 95, 96, and 97. Train 94 was labeled the *Peoria Time Freight,* train 96 was called the *Peoria–St. Louis Flour Special,* and trains 95 and 97 were both hailed as the *Twin Cities Time Freight.*[39]

Freight volume on Iowa Central was most intense between Mason City and Marshalltown, where, in addition to the two time freights, the

Figure 9.29. Iowa Central eagerly solicited special movements such as Redpath's Chautauqua train, which left Oskaloosa on August 5, 1907. Note the road's handsome depot in the background.

Figure 9.30. The pastoral setting of Winfield seemed more appropriate to Iowa Central than its grand station facility at Oskaloosa.

Figure 9.31. Train 3, a maid-of-all-work run between Peoria and Mason City, paused each midafternoon before the depot at New Sharon. The girl about to walk in front of the locomotive on her way home or elsewhere seems quite unimpressed with the hubbub on the station platform—a routine practiced to perfection across the land during the steamcar civilization. Vaughn R. Ward collection.

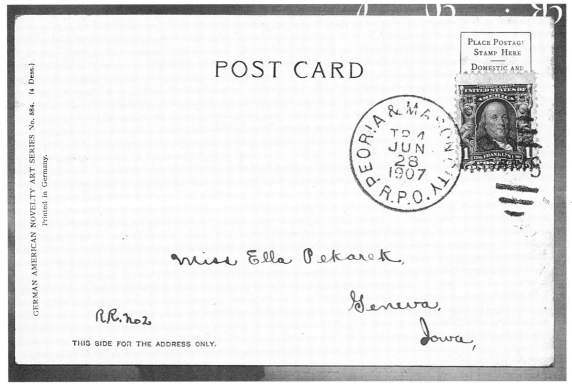

Figure 9.32. Mail was heavy on Peoria & Mason City Railway Post Office train 3. Postcards like this one were handed to clerks who applied cancellations (postmarks) and directed them to their destinations through an intricate national web known as the Railway Mail Service.

Figure 9.33. Train 2 connected at Albert Lea with M&StL service from Minneapolis and worked Iowa Central's line to Albia. There was time to spare this day—or the crew took the time—to pose for this image at Sheffield. Vaughn R. Ward collection.

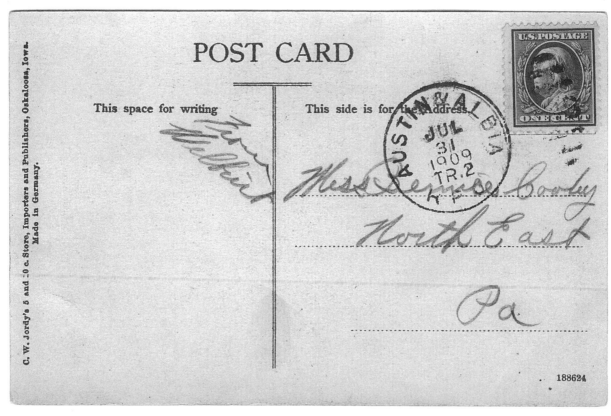

Figure 9.34. Iowa Central and its predecessors for many years had participated in through passenger arrangements with Chicago, Milwaukee & St. Paul via Mason City Junction, and even after that Railway Post Office (RPO) assignments on Iowa Central train 2 started at Austin (the point of origin) on a Milwaukee train that continued to connect with Iowa Central at Mason City Junction. Thus on Iowa Central there was the curiosity of two RPO lines—Austin & Albia and Peoria & Mason City—assigned over its trackage between Oskaloosa and Mason City.

Central operated a daily-except-Sunday stock train from Mason City to Marshalltown and a daily-except-Sunday time freight between Marshalltown and Hampton. These were supplemented by way freights. Freight traffic was lighter between Marshalltown and Oskaloosa, where regular through freight trains plus way freights combined to offer four daily in each direction. From Oskaloosa to Albia the company operated two each way, and from Oskaloosa to Peoria four in each direction. In addition to regularly scheduled movements, the road frequently operated extras on all lines to move any backlog of traffic—especially for coal and grain.[40]

During the late summer of 1911, President Newman Erb predicted that Iowa Central soon would extend its rails from Albia to St. Louis, and Iowa Central and M&StL officials prowled Fort Dodge, Des Moines & Southern, apparently with the idea of acquiring its line from Newton to Des Moines Junction as a logical extension of Iowa Central's Newton Branch, or maybe even with the thought of taking all of that infant railroad. Erb's comments and the comings and goings of Hawley men encouraged the on-line press to speculate as to Hawley's ultimate goals. In any event, it was obvious even to the most casual observer of the railroad scene that Iowa Central soon would be merged into the Minneapolis & St. Louis Railroad. Chairman Hawley had directed that large sums of money be spent on the main line of the Central, and substantial right-of-way and motive power

Figure 9.35. Passenger trains got the public's attention, but freight paid the bills. Pickering, where the crew of this local freight had paused from the routine of station work, was one of dozens of important way stations forwarding agricultural produce and receiving a bewildering array of consumer goods—everything from caskets to corsets. Vaughn R. Ward collection.

Figure 9.36. The crew of an eastbound passenger train took time to have their picture recorded at Hedrick. Amos Garrett was on the engineer's seatbox, and John Chase, station agent, had his right hand on the locomotive's pilot. Soon they would be M&StL employees. Vaughn R. Ward collection.

upgrading had been accomplished. In addition, the Central and M&StL had been working closely on traffic matters for some years. Late in 1911 Hawley, at Erb's insistence, decided that the time had come.[41]

On December 18, 1911, a special meeting was held, and the Central's stockholders decided, not surprisingly, to sell the entire property of the Iowa Central Railway to M&StL. Simultaneously, M&StL's stockholders approved the purchase of Iowa Central. Financial arrangements stipulated that the Central would turn over its entire property plus $2,500,000 in cash for $9,370,000 in M&StL common stock, $1,917,500 in preferred stock, and $2,500,000 in "refunding and extension mortgage

5 p.c. 50 year gold bonds." The basis of exchange was as follows:

1. $900.00 (par) of common and $100.00 (par) of preferred stock of this company [M&StL] for $1,000.00 (par) of preferred stock of the Iowa Central Railway Company.
2. $100.00 (par) of common stock of this Company [M&StL] for $200.00 (par) of common stock of the Iowa Central Railway Company.

These arrangements were accepted by all parties, and at 12:01 a.m. on January 1, 1912, the Iowa Central Railway ceased to exist as a corporate entity.[42]

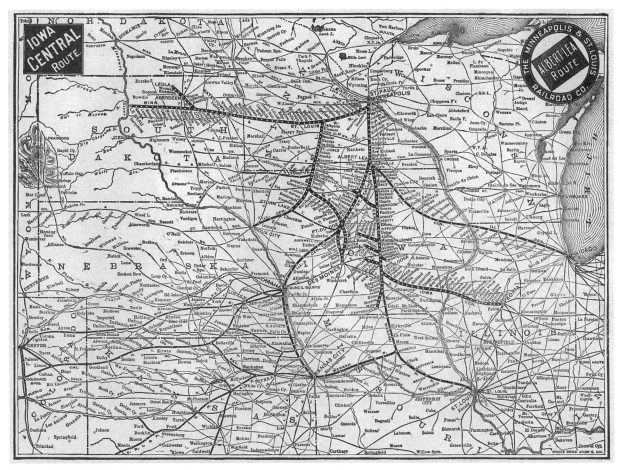

Map 9.3. The merged Iowa Central and M&StL.

EPILOGUE

Mergers represent the natural tendency of railroad corporations toward unification of interests.
—COLLIS P. HUNTINGTON, "A PLEA FOR RAILROAD CONSOLIDATION"

IT WAS INEVITABLE. FROM THE DAYS OF THE Eldora Railroad & Coal Company, the managers of that company and of the companies that evolved into Iowa Central had known that the property would have to expand or be absorbed. Cut off at both the northern and the southern borders of Iowa, it would be only a local road, the line out to Peoria notwithstanding. Its fight for survival was a long one and a good one; its several management teams showed remarkable ingenuity in keeping the operation independent for nearly a half century.

Consolidation of Minneapolis & St. Louis and Iowa Central constituted an "end-to-end" merger, with the lines of one complementing the lines of the other to create a relatively vibrant north–south railroad. And the new system might have become a major segment of Edwin Hawley's audacious scheme to create a major vertical-axis route from Canada to the Gulf of Mexico. Fate intervened, however. Edwin Hawley died unexpectedly one month after M&StL and Iowa Central merged. Once a member of the "Waldorf Crowd" that included "Diamond Jim" Brady, "Bet-a-Million" Gates, George Crocker, Dan Sully, and Bernard

Baruch, Hawley was, as one observer put it, "in no sense of the word an educated man." Yet when he died, he was an acknowledged master in the railroad world and a dominant figure in high finance. Now he was gone. So, too, was his daring strategic plan.[1]

Owners of the newly merged M&StL–Iowa Central company expected that it would be a profitable enterprise. Financial success eluded the road, however, and on July 26, 1923, it plunged into receivership. M&StL failed to show a profit during the remainder of the 1920s, and with the stock market crash of 1929 and the Great Depression of the 1930s, the company's financial burdens compounded. Fortunately for M&StL, a "Doctor of Sick Railroads," Lucian C. Sprague, was summoned; his prescriptions and elixirs transformed "Maimed & Still Limping," as M&StL was mockingly referred to, into "Modern & Streamlined." It was reorganized without funded debt on December 1, 1943.[2]

The rehabilitation process ordered by Sprague was as successful as it was rigorous. The main line from Minneapolis to Peoria was greatly improved, and the road gained fame for its expeditious move-

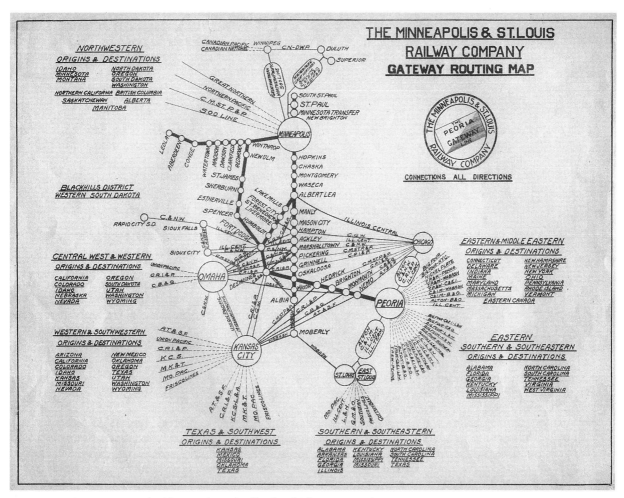

Map E.1. M&StL, now merged with Iowa Central, offered multiple routing options.

ment of freight—avoiding, as it did, the congestion of Chicago. At the same time that Sprague and crew were building up the Peoria Gateway, they turned to dry-eyed analysis of expensive or unprofitable operations. Passenger service was trimmed to the bone; not even the *North Star Limited* was spared. Next came abandonment of Iowa Central's main line between Martinsburg and Coppock, which was replaced with a better alignment acquired from Chicago, Burlington & Quincy in 1934–35 when it terminated operation of what once had been the pesky narrow gauge that paralleled Iowa Central.[3]

Branch lines also fell under the hammer. The historic Montezuma Branch was taken up in 1936.

The State Center Branch had been cut back to Van Cleve during the 1920s, was further trimmed to Laurel during the 1940s, and was finally abandoned from Newburg to Laurel in the 1950s. The Algona Branch suffered a similar fate. Service initially was reduced to St. Benedict, then to Corwith, next to Denhardt, and eventually to Kanawha. The Story City Branch was cut back to Roland in the 1950s, and the Newton Branch perished in 1962.[4]

M&StL enjoyed financial success throughout the 1940s and the 1950s. It paid regular dividends, carried little debt, and became a luscious plum ready to be picked by an opportunistic raider. In a bitter proxy fight in 1954, Lucian Sprague, the man who had saved M&StL from destruction, was

Figure E.1. Former Iowa Central employees at Marshalltown found little difference in operations under M&StL ownership. Nor was there much difference in motive power, which was still modest in the extreme, as this M&StL 4-4-0 at the Marshalltown engine facility suggests.

Figure E.2. Freight business was good—very good indeed—during World War II. Here an M&StL 2-8-2 was lugging tonnage west from Peoria to Maxwell on May 6, 1944. David Lewis photograph.

Figure E.3. Marshalltown retained primary switching assignments on the former Iowa Central, and the primary shops were there, but Oskaloosa shared important responsibilities. Dispatchers were housed in the large, attractive depot seen at the upper left, and minor repairs and considerable switching were done at the Mahaska County seat. In this photo handsome M&StL Mikado 634 headed south toward Albia with tonnage for Wabash on April 23, 1949. Robert Milner photograph.

Figure E.4. In 1948, modern diesel-electric locomotives hurried M&StL's famous time freight 19 through Eldora, where the Iowa Central story had begun with the formation of the Eldora Railroad & Coal Company.

Figure E.5. Winds of change. A blend of colors on these locomotives denotes M&StL's new ownership, Chicago & North Western. Marshalltown, April 1962.

ousted by a group headed by Ben W. Heineman. Then on November 1, 1960, Heineman merged the Minneapolis & St. Louis Railway into another of his "plums"—the Chicago & North Western System.[5]

So it was that trackage of the former Iowa Central, "that orphan railroad . . . wooed and jilted by interests from the Hawkeye State to Wall Street," switched hands again. The transaction reflected an industry-wide pattern driven by a changed and changing transportation landscape characterized by fierce modal competition from pipelines, waterways, automobiles, trucks, and airlines. The age of the railways clearly was now past. Early casualties included local passenger service and less-than-carload freight, followed by long-distance passenger trains and highly rated merchandise and other boxcar freight. The result was silent depots and

rusting switch stands—mute reminders of an era, not long removed, when communities large and small had been wholly dependent on railroads for transportation.

The march of change was relentless. Merger was the nostrum of choice. During the 1990s Chicago & North Western itself disappeared into the bowels of giant Union Pacific. By the twenty-first century only bits and pieces of the former Iowa Central remained—Northwood–Manly, Mason City–Rockwell, Geneva–Eddyville, and Middle Grove–Peoria as well as the Belmond–Kanawha portion of what once had been the Algona Branch. Of these, Northwood–Manly had vital strategic importance for Union Pacific, and Marshalltown–Eddyville provided service for a major shipper at Eddyville; the rest faced an uncertain future.[6]

Sic gloria transit.

Figure E.6. Dismantlers took up track on the former main line west of Oakville, near "old" Newport. May 16, 1972.

NOTES

1. Urban Mercantilism

1. G. R. Taylor, *Transportation Revolution*, vii, 396–98; Martin, *Railroads Triumphant*, 201.

2. Blegen, *Minnesota*, 159–73, 180; G. R. Taylor, *Transportation Revolution*, 388–89; John F. Stover, *American Railroads*, 1–34.

3. King, "John Plumbe," 289–96; Johnson, "Plumbe's Railroad," 89–97; Francaviglia and Bryan, "'Are We Chimerical?'" 179–202.

4. Boeck, "Transportation Fever," 129–52; Meyer, *Railway Legislation*, 3, 6.

5. Lea, quoted in Cole, *Iowa through the Years*, 170; Cole, *Iowa through the Years*, 45–52, 106–8, 119–23, 192–215; Wall, *Iowa*, 24–26; *Andreas Atlas*, 404–5.

6. On the general topic, see Stover, *Iron Road;* Primm, *Lion of the Valley*, 9, 49, 73, 107–13, 165–69; Cronon, *Nature's Metropolis*, 26, 60–68, 110–15, 298–309.

7. Glaab, *Kansas City and the Railroads*, 124–25; Primm, *Lion of the Valley*, 201; Cronon, *Nature's Metropolis*, 298–309; Taylor and Neu, *American Railroad Network*, 40–41.

8. Primm, *Lion of the Valley*, 9, 49, 73, 107, 113, 165–69.

9. Stover, *Iron Road*, ix, 13, 16, 116; Casey and Douglas, *Pioneer Railroad*, 3–89, 308–9; Grant, *The North Western*, 3–24; Hayes, *Iron Road*, 21–30; Agnew, "Rock Island Lines," 407–24; Stover, *Illinois Central*, 54–56; Corliss, *Main Line*, 21–69; Overton, *Burlington Route*, 41–43; Cary, *Chicago, Milwaukee & St. Paul Railway*, 8, 378.

10. On the first transcontinental road, see Ambrose, *Nothing Like It;* and Bain, *Empire Express; Yesterday and Today*, 40; Branch, "The North Western," 212–18; Baldwin, *The Chicago, Burlington & Quincy Railroad*, 343; Chicago, Rock Island & Pacific, Annual Report, 1870, p. 5; Hayes, *Iron Road*, pp. 49–57; Overton, *Burlington Route*, 78–96.

2. Iowa Central Railroad

1. The Iowa Central Railroad should not be confused with either the Iowa Central Railway, an operating company that passed to the Minneapolis & St. Louis Railroad in 1912, or the Iowa Central Air Line Railroad, a paper company. On the Iowa Central Air Line, see Casey and Douglas, *Pioneer Railroad*, 124–25, and Preston, "The Lyons and Iowa Central," 284–301. Portions of this chapter appeared as "The Greatest Railroad Project of the Age," *Annals of Iowa* 44 (Fall 1977): 118–36.

2. *Organization and Articles of Incorporation of the Iowa Central R.R. Co.* (Des Moines: Iowa State Register Printing, 1866), available at the University of Iowa Library, Iowa City. Hereinafter referred to as *Organization . . . Iowa Central R.R;* Payne, *Josiah Bushnell Grinnell*, 61.

3. Wright, *Peter Melendy*, 255; *Organization . . . Iowa Central R.R.*, 5; Gates, "Railroads of Missouri," 126–41.

4. *Organization . . . Iowa Central R.R,* 12–13; *Cedar Falls Gazette,* July 14 and August 11, 1865, January 12, 1866.

5. *Cedar Falls Gazette,* July 7 and August 11, 1865, January 5, 1866, February 8, 1867; *Organization . . . Iowa Central R.R.,* 15–16. For an assessment of this rivalry see Belcher, *Economic Rivalry,* and Adler, *Yankee Merchants.*

6. *Organization . . . Iowa Central R.R.,* 11–13; *Cedar Falls Gazette,* July 7 and August 25, 1865. See also Beard, "Local Aid to Railroads," 19–22.

7. *Cedar Falls Gazette,* July 7, 1865, February 8 and November 1, 1867. See also Beard, "State Railroad Regulations," 1–36, esp. 20.

8. *Cedar Falls Gazette,* July 7 and August 11, 1865, March 22 and October 25, 1867; *Organization . . . Iowa Central R.R.,* 12–13.

9. *Organization . . . Iowa Central R.R.,* 12–13, 20; *Cedar Falls Gazette,* March 9 and 23, April 13, and May 4, 1866; U.S. House of Representatives, 39th Congress, 1st Session, 1865–66, *Miscellaneous Documents,* 3 vols., vol. 3, Misc. Doc. no. 76 (n.d.).

10. S. Chamberlain, president of the Minnesota Central Railway, letter to Peter Melendy, March 5, 1866, reproduced in the April 27, 1866, issue of the *Cedar Falls Gazette;* William R. Marshall, governor of Minnesota, letter to Peter Melendy, May 19, 1866, reproduced in the June 1, 1866, issue of the *Cedar Falls Gazette;* Wright, *Peter Melendy,* 248.

11. *Cedar Falls Gazette,* September 1, 1865; *St. Louis Democrat,* undated article reproduced in the *Cedar Falls Gazette,* July 21, 1865; Cronon, *Nature's Metropolis,* 295–309; Primm, *Lion of the Valley,* 270–71, 280, 287–97.

12. *Cedar Falls Gazette,* June 30, 1865; *Organization . . . Iowa Central R.R.,* 12 13.

13. *Cedar Falls Gazette,* September 22, 1865; Wright, *Peter Melendy,* 237–39.

14. *Organization . . . Iowa Central R.R.,* 5; *Cedar Falls Gazette,* September 15, November 3 and 10, 1865, September 7 and 28, 1866, March 1, 1967.

15. Wright, *Peter Melendy,* 241; *Oskaloosa Herald,* undated article reproduced in the *Cedar Falls Gazette,* December 22, 1865.

16. *Organization . . . Iowa Central R.R.,* 12–13; *Cedar Falls Gazette,* April 13 and June 1, 1866; George W.

Blood, secretary of the North Missouri Railroad, letter to William P. Smith, March 15, 1866, reproduced in the *Cedar Falls Gazette,* March 20, 1866.

17. *Albia Union,* May 17, 1866; *Oskaloosa Herald,* June 28, 1866; *Cedar Falls Gazette,* May 25 and July 27, November 30, December 7 and 28, 1866.

18. *Report of the (Iowa) Board of Railroad Commissioners,* 1896, 220–21; *Cedar Falls Gazette,* May 4 and June 15, 1866, May 3, 1867; "Articles of Incorporation of the Iowa Central Railroad Construction Company," available at the office of the Iowa Secretary of State, Des Moines.

19. *Cedar Falls Gazette,* August 4 and 11, September 1, 1865.

20. *Report of the (Iowa) Board of Railroad Commissioners,* 1880, 246–47; ibid., 1896, 186–87.

21. *Cedar Falls Gazette,* April 13 and 27, June 8, July 27, December 28, 1866; Taylor and Neu, *American Railroad Network,* 40–41.

22. *St. Louis Times,* undated story reproduced in the *Cedar Falls Gazette,* May 3, 1867; *St. Louis Republican,* October 18, 1867, a story reproduced in the *Cedar Falls Gazette,* October 25, 1867.

23. Swartz, "Wabash Railroad," 33; *Cedar Falls Gazette,* September 13, 1867.

24. *Cedar Falls Gazette,* March 22, July 12, September 13, 1867; William T. Smith, undated letter to the editor of the *St. Louis Times,* reproduced in the *Cedar Falls Gazette,* May 3, 1867; *St. Louis Republican,* undated story reproduced in the *Cedar Falls Gazette,* November 8, 1867.

25. *Cedar Falls Gazette,* May 3, 1867, April 24, 1868; *St. Louis Republican,* undated story reproduced in the *Cedar Falls Gazette,* August 14, 1868.

26. *Cedar Falls Gazette,* April 3, 1868, April 16, 1869; Beard, "State Railroad Regulations," 24; Swartz, "Wabash Railroad," 9; Wright, *Peter Melendy,* 245; *Toledo Chronicle,* December 7, 1950; Belcher, *Economic Rivalry,* 125; *Report of the (Iowa) Board of Railroad Commissioners,* 1880, 246–47; Donovan, "Wabash in Iowa," 369–74; Reavis, *Railway and River Systems,* 212–25.

27. *Central Railroad of Iowa: Value and Security of Its Bonds,* September 15, 1869, Bureau of Economics Library, Association of American Railroads, Washington.

3. Eldora Railroad & Coal Company

1. *Eldora Ledger,* January 10, 1866. Portions of this chapter appeared as "The Railroad and an Iowa Editor: A Case Study," *Annals of Iowa* 41 (Fall 1972): 1073–1103.

2. *History of Hardin County,* 233.

3. Ibid., 639.

4. *Iowa Board of Railroad Commissioners Report,* 1896, 221; *Cedar Falls Gazette,* May 19, 1865.

5. *History of Hardin County,* 506; *Eldora Ledger,* January 31, 1866. According to the *History of Hardin County* the company was chartered on February 7, 1866 (p. 506); on Platt Smith, see Cochran, *Railroad Leaders,* 461–66, and Larson, "Platt Smith," 88–96.

6. *Eldora Ledger,* May 23, 1866.

7. Ibid., January 20, 1867.

8. *History of Hardin County,* 507; *Eldora Ledger,* February 6, 1867.

9. *Eldora Ledger,* February 20, 1867; *Cedar Falls Gazette,* February 22, 1867.

10. *History of Hardin County,* 507.

11. *Eldora Ledger,* February 20, March 6 and 13, 1867.

12. *History of Hardin County,* 507; *Eldora Ledger,* June 26, 1867.

13. *Eldora Ledger,* July 3 and 24, August 7, September 11, 1867.

14. Corliss, *Main Line,* 150; *Eldora Ledger,* October 9 and November 6, 1867; Bennett and McLintock, "M&StL Railroad Co. History," 7.

15. *Eldora Ledger,* October 30, 1867.

16. Ibid., January 11 and February 29, 1868.

17. Ibid., March 28 and April 11, 1868.

18. Prospectus of the Eldora Railroad & Coal Company, 1866, quoted in *History of Hardin County,* 339; *Eldora Ledger,* May 16, 1868.

19. *Eldora Ledger,* May 16 and 23, 1868.

20. Ibid., May 30 and June 20, 1868; *Cedar Falls Gazette,* March 24, 1867.

21. *Eldora Ledger,* May 30, June 6, 13, and 27, July 4, 1868.

22. Ibid., June 13, 1868.

23. Ibid., June 20, 1868. Departure from Steamboat Rock was scheduled for 4:50 a.m. and 5:40 p.m.; departure from Steamboat Rock was set for 7:15 a.m. and 7:15 p.m.

24. *Eldora Ledger,* June 27, July 4, 1868.

25. Ibid., May 23, June 6 and 20, 1868.

26. Ibid., July 11, 1868.

27. Ibid.

28. Ibid.

29. Ibid.; *History of Hardin County,* 507. There was a similar celebration at the opposite end of the line, where a dance was held at the Ackley House. See *Ackley World Journal,* "Centennial Edition," August 1, 1957; *Eldora Ledger,* August 1, 1866. Jonathan Gilman may or may not have been related to Charles Gilman.

30. *Eldora Ledger,* August 8 and 22, September 19, 1868; Iowa River Railway, Prospectus (1869), 26. Articles of incorporation were filed July 8, 1868, but it is not clear when full control of the railroad portion of the Eldora Railroad & Coal Company passed to the Iowa River Railway. By mid-September the *Eldora Ledger* was referring to the railroad as the Iowa River Road rather than the Eldora Road.

31. *Eldora Ledger,* August 29 and September 19, 1868.

4. Iowa River Railway

1. *History of Hardin County,* 512–13; Corliss, *Main Line,* 151–53. For additional information on the Dubuque bridge see Leland L. Sage, *William Boyd Allison,* 78.

2. *History of Marshall County,* 418; *History of Hardin County,* 513; Iowa River Railway, Prospectus, 12.

3. Iowa River Railway, Prospectus, 26.

4. Ibid., 3, 13. Isaac Hyde Jr. replaced H. P. Liscomb, who died just at the time the Iowa River Railroad was being incorporated.

5. Iowa River Railway, Prospectus, 5, 13.

6. Battin and Moscrip, *Past and Present of Marshall County,* vol. 1, 201–2.

7. Ibid.; *History of Hardin County,* 508. Abraham Stanley and John W. Tripp, residents of what was then Iowa Township, were jointly responsible for raising $20,000 from the area that now embraces the towns of Albion and Liscomb. Marshalltown subscribed for the remaining $60,000.

8. Iowa River Railway, Prospectus, 3.

9. Ibid., 1 (map).

10. Ibid., 4–5.

11. Ibid., 24.

12. Ibid., 26.

13. Ibid., 26–27; Means, "Minneapolis & St. Louis Railroad Company," 13.

14. Iowa River Railway, Prospectus, p. 28.

15. *Report of the (Iowa) Board of Railroad Commissioners,* 1896, 223.

16. Bennett and McLintock, "M&StL Railroad Co. History," 7; *Report of the (Iowa) Board of Railroad Commissioners,* 1896, 23. There is some question as to whether the River road had determined the exact route to the north. Later documents indicate the desire of the road to build north to Hampton, Nora Springs, and the state line from that point. However, it does seem certain that Hampton had been the initial goal as the line built north from Ackley.

5. Central Railroad Company of Iowa

1. Central Railroad Company of Iowa, Value and Security of Its First Mortgage Seven Per Cent Gold Bonds, September 15, 1869, 33; Bennett and McLintock, "M&StL Railroad Co. History," 4, 21.

2. Central Railroad Company of Iowa, Articles of Incorporation, 6.

3. Central Railroad Company of Iowa, Value and Security, September 15, 1869, 33.

4. Ibid., 1.

5. Central Railroad Company of Iowa, Articles of Incorporation, 9.

6. *Report of the (Iowa) Board of Railroad Commissioners,* 1896, 223; *History of Marshall County,* 419.

7. Bennett and McLintock, "M&StL Railroad Co. History," 4; Central Railroad Company of Iowa, Value and Security, September 15, 1869, 6, 11, 34.

8. Central Railroad Company of Iowa, Value and Security, March 1, 1870, 10; *Minneapolis Tribune,* August 2, 1872.

9. These twenty-three miles of grade extended from Ackley to a community now called Chapin. Apparently this was the point at which a decision had to be made. The grade could go toward Nora Springs as originally planned or toward Mason City without any loss or circuitous routing.

10. Central Railroad Company of Iowa, Value and Security, June 20, 1870, 10; Stuart, *History of Franklin County,* vol. 1, 233.

11. Stuart, *History of Franklin County,* vol. 1, 233–35; Foster, *Franklin County History,* 33–36.

12. Central Railroad Company of Iowa, Value and Security, June 20, 1870, 10; Enoch A. Norem (compiler), "The Mason City Story," Centennial Edition, *Mason City Globe-Gazette,* July 1, 1953.

13. Central Railroad Company of Iowa, Value and Security, October 1, 1870, 2; *Report of the (Iowa) Board of Railroad Commissioners,* 1896, 209; Central Railroad Company of Iowa, Value and Security, March 1, 1870, 10.

14. *History of Monroe County,* 453; Hickenlooper, *Illustrated History of Monroe County,* 130; Central Railroad Company of Iowa, Value and Security, September 15, 1869, 28.

15. Central Railroad Company of Iowa, Value and Security, June 20, 1870, 2, 10.

16. *Minneapolis Tribune,* May 17, 1871; Donovan, "Wabash in Iowa," 371.

17. *Minneapolis Tribune,* December 4, 1870; Grinnell, *Men and Events of Forty Years,* 301; Parker, *History of Poweshiek County,* 150; news item in the *Poweshiek County Herald* date unknown (December 1870). A clipping of the latter was found in a scrapbook at Grinnell College Library, Grinnell, Iowa.

18. *History of Mahaska County* (1878), 345; *Grinnell Herald-Register,* May 22, 1958.

19. *Grinnell Herald-Register,* May 22, 1958.

20. The *Grinnell Herald-Register,* May 22, 1958, citing a piece by editor J. M. Chamberlain of the *Poweshiek County Journal* in its February 8, 1871, issue, noted that "a telegraph wire was attached to the polished spike and another wrapped around the hammer which was to send it home, so that the electric circle was made complete when the hammer rested on the spike. Each tap was heard by friends in New York"; *History of Mahaska County* (1878), 347; Central Railroad Company of Iowa, Report of Earnings for the Month of October, 1871, 12; *History of Hardin County,* 513–14.

21. *Grinnell Herald-Register,* May 22, 1958.

22. *Marshalltown Times-Republican,* Centennial Edition, June 30, 1953.

23. *History of Mitchell and Worth Counties,* 698–99; Bennett and McLintock, "M&StL Railroad Co. History," 7.

24. There is some evidence that the Central gave a goodly amount of traffic to Des Moines Valley (DMV) at Givin (four miles north of Eddyville) and to Burlington & Missouri River (B&MR) at Maxon near Albia. It is possible that the Central Railroad Company of Iowa (CRCI) operated passenger trains over B&MR from Maxon to Ottumwa for a very brief period. Later on, through service did move to Ottumwa via Givin and a DMV successor for a lengthy period. *Official Guide,* May 1876, 409.

25. *Minneapolis Tribune,* August 24, September 8 and 19, 1872.

26. Many of the facilities at Marshalltown were consumed in a devastating fire that delayed full use of centralized shopping at that point. Central Railroad Company of Iowa, Report of the Boston Committee to Bondholders, 22.

27. Ibid., 23.

28. Ibid., 28; Central Railroad Company of Iowa, Weekly Local Ticket Report.

29. Central Railroad Company of Iowa, Report of the Boston Committee to Bondholders, 20–21; *Poor's Manual,* 1883, 786.

30. Fels, *American Business Cycles,* 97.

6. The Tangled Ways of Finance

1. *Poor's Manual,* 1883, 786.

2. *History of Mahaska County* (1878), 520.

3. Donovan, *Mileposts,* 28; Welles, *Autobiography and Reminiscences,* vol. 2, 139; Oberholtzer, *Jay Cooke,* vol. 1, 92–95, 168, 350–51; Smalley, *Northern Pacific Railroad,* 97, 101, 102; Northern Pacific Railroad, Report of the Chief Engineer on the Unfinished Portion, April 27, 1874, 1.

4. *Report of the (Iowa) Board of Railroad Commissioners,* 1896, 186; *Minneapolis Tribune,* January 9, 1872.

5. *Poor's Manual,* 1874, 453.

6. Central Railroad Company of Iowa, Report of the Boston Committee to Bondholders, 1.

7. Ibid., 1; Sarnoff, *Russell Sage,* 172.

8. Central Railroad Company of Iowa, Report of the Boston Committee to Bondholders, 3. The grading of this four-mile stretch had been finished in 1871.

9. The New York Committee did not entirely exclude the possibility of a lease to some strong carrier. However, the New Yorkers indicated a willingness to lease the property only as a last resort.

10. Central Railroad Company of Iowa, Report of the Boston Committee to Bondholders, 10–11.

11. Ibid., 35. The influence of Gilman and the other Iowa bondholders can be seen in the fact that the new company proposed to establish Eldora as its principal place of business. It is interesting to note that the New York group sought an additional outlet to the north (probably Minneapolis & St. Louis) for the Central's traffic, while the Boston Committee, with the "intangible support" of Russell Sage and the Milwaukee & St. Paul Railroad (which effected a through connection to the east and the north via Mason City), proposed building a twenty-seven-mile spur from Albia to Moulton to gain a direct connection with the St. Louis, Kansas City, & Northern (successor to the North Missouri and a Gould-Sage Company). However, the Boston Committee wanted to lease or sell the property without building another mile of line.

12. Central Railroad Company of Iowa, Report of the Boston Committee to Bondholders, 29.

13. Central Railroad Company of Iowa, Compromise Measure, 5.

14. Ibid., 1.

15. St. Louis, Iowa and Minnesota R.R. Co., Prospectus, 21; Grinnell, *Men and Events of Forty Years,* 302.

16. The "old" Boston Committee had been highly critical of receiver D. N. Pickering during the time that the Boston and New York groups were in disagreement. With the leadership of both groups now combined under the banner of the Joint Committee, the old Boston Committee members must have viewed the defense of Pickering with tongue in cheek.

17. Grinnell, *Men and Events of Forty Years,* 303.

18. *Men and Events of Forty Years,* 303–5.

19. Ibid.

20. "How Eli Got There," a story in a scrapbook belonging to Mary Hutchins, Pasadena, California,

a distant relative of J. B. Grinnell. Copy of file at the Grinnell College Library.

21. Central Railroad Company of Iowa, Receivers Report, 3–4.

22. Cate, representing the Joint Committee, lashed out at Grinnell in a series of oral as well as written attacks.

23. Grinnell, *Men and Events of Forty Years,* 304.

24. Ibid. Even James Grant, solicitor for the plaintiff (Farmers Loan & Trust), in a suit to discharge Grinnell's bondsmen, had this to say: "Upon his surrender of the property, I concur entirely in the opinions of the State Commissioners that he has very much improved the conditions of the same, and he left it in far superior condition to that in which he received it."

25. Donovan, *Mileposts,* 109.

26. *Report of the (Iowa) Board of Railroad Commissioners,* 1896, 186.

27. *History of Mitchell and Worth Counties,* 700.

28. Neill, *History of Freeborn County,* 355; *Report of the (Iowa) Board of Railway Commissioners,* 1896, 187. M&StL paid for building the line from Albert Lea to the Iowa border.

7. The Hook & Eye

1. Bennett and McLintock, "M&StL Railroad Co. History," 4; *Poor's Manual,* 1880, 846; *Iowa Board of Railroad Commissioners Report,* 1896, 244.

2. *Iowa Board of Railroad Commissioners Report,* 1879, 299.

3. Bennett and McLintock, "M&StL Railroad Co. History," 24, *Railroad Gazette,* August 16, 1873, 335.

4. *History of Poweshiek County,* 515; *Official Guide,* May 1876, 409,

5. Grinnell, *Men and Events of Forty Years,* 300. *Iowa Board of Railroad Commissioners Report,* 1878, 262.

6. *Biographical and Historical Memoirs,* 180.

7. Bennett and McLintock, "M&StL Railroad Co. History," 22; *Belmond Independent,* July 30, 1925.

8. *Belmond Independent,* July 30, 1925; *Belmond Herald,* November 2, 1881.

9. *Belmond Herald,* November 2, 1881.

10. Bennett and McLintock, "M&StL Railroad Co. History," 3, 22.

11. Ibid., 4; Central Iowa Railway, Annual Report, 1882, 6–9.

12. Central Iowa Railway, Annual Report, 1882, 6–9; *Report of the (Iowa) Board of Railroad Commissioners,* 1883, 235.

13. Bray interview.

14. Heninger interview.

15. Wilson, "Narrow Gauge," 152; Lotz, "The Burlington Lines," 4–27; *Railroad Gazette,* April 28, 1882, 261.

16. Heacock, *Local Reminiscences,* 102; Hilton, *American Narrow Gauge Railroads,* 394–95.

17. Heacock, *Local Reminiscences,* 105; Lota and Franzen, *Rails to a County Seat,* 28–51.

18. *Iowa Board of Railroad Commissioners Report,* 1883, 235; Bennett and McLintock, "M&StL Railroad Co. History," 21. The Trunk Line Construction Company was headed by Alfred Sully, a crony of Russell Sage.

19. Bennett and McLintock, "M&StL Railroad Co. History," 22; Central Iowa Railway, Annual Report, 1882, 8–9.

20. Sturm, "Railroads and Market Growth," 53–54, 76–79, 108–9, 121, 126–31, 137–38.

21. Minneapolis & St. Louis, Search of Records Document; Havinghurst, *Land of Promise,* 203–4; Davis, "Illinois," 127–57.

22. Illinois Railroad and Warehouse Commission, Annual Report, 1883, 15.

23. Ibid., 22; *History of Mercer County,* 170; Illinois Railroad and Warehouse Commission, Annual Report, 1875, 58.

24. Illinois Railroad and Warehouse Commission, Annual Report, 1879, 75.

25. *Portrait of Warren County,* 806.

26. Ibid., 510.

27. Stringham letter, citing newspaper files in the Peoria Library.

28. Bennett and McLintock, "M&StL Railroad Co. History," 5; Stringham letter.

29. Stringham letter.

30. Bennett and McLintock, "M&StL Railroad Co. History," 6; Stringham letter. In *Past and Present of Mercer County, Illinois,* Isaac N. Bassett theorizes that the railroads sought Keithsburg because it would offer an excellent location for a river-rail interchange facility, because

there was an active lumber industry that would contribute considerable revenue traffic, because it was a good grain shipping point, and because the sand and gravel quarried in this locale was in demand over a large area.

31. Bennett and McLintock, "M&StL Railroad Co. History," 3; Haynes, "History of Bridge."

32. Haynes, "History of Bridge."

33. Stringham letter.

34. Haynes, "History of Bridge"; Bennett and McLintock, "M&StL Railroad Co. History," 6. The Railroad Commissioners of Iowa noted in their report for the year 1884 that the Central paid out $13,030.04 for Mississippi River transfer charges.

35. Haynes, "History of Bridge"; *Chicago Tribune,* February 23, 1886.

36. Haynes, "History of Bridge."

37. *History of Mitchell and Worth Counties,* 700; *Minneapolis Tribune,* February 22, 1889.

38. Lewis, *History of Appanoose and Monroe Counties,* 15.

39. Taylor, *Past and Present of Appanoose County,* 261; Donovan, "Wabash in Iowa," 387; Grodinsky, *Jay Gould,* 244. On Gould, see also Klein, *Jay Gould.*

40. Donovan, *Mileposts,* 115.

41. Ibid., 106.

42. Ibid.

43. *History of Mahaska County* (1984), 316.

44. Central Railroad Company of Iowa, Memorandum Guide.

45. Chicago, Milwaukee & St. Paul et al., Time Schedule. Actually the Central joined Keokuk & Des Moines about four miles north of Eddyville, with the respective stations simply across town from each other.

46. Minnesota & Northwestern was a predecessor of Chicago Great Western Railroad. On that company, see Grant, *Corn Belt Route; Official Guide,* 344; *Official Guide,* December 1889, 396.

47. Donovan, *Mileposts,* 114. Until February 1, 1884, Central Iowa Railway's passenger trains used Chicago, Burlington & Quincy's depot at Peoria. However, after that date Central Iowa trains used Peoria & Pekin Union Railroad's Union Station.

48. Central Iowa Railway, Time Table, May 2, 1886.

49. Hoffman, *Oskaloosa,* 14–16, 67; *History of Mahaska County* (1984), 53; *Official Guide,* June 1884,

238; Central Iowa Railway, Time Table, August 24, 1884, map.

50. Central Iowa Railway, *The Great Northwest,* passim.

51. *Poor's Manual,* 1886, 951.

52. Ibid., 1886, 498; Alvin F. Harlow, *Steelways of New England,* 427; Donovan, "Amazing Great Western," 15.

53. *Minneapolis Tribune,* January 30, 1889; *Railway World,* September 11, 1880; *New York Times,* September 23, 1882; *Boston Transcript,* August 19 and 28, 1885; *Railroad Gazette,* February 21, 1886, 154.

54. *Poor's Manual,* 1887, 804.

55. Interstate Commerce Commission, *Valuation Reports,* vol. 137, 870–78; Bennett and McLintock, "M&StL Railroad Co. History," 6.

56. *Iowa Board of Railroad Commissioners Report,* 1896, 225.

8. Iowa Central Railway

1. *Iowa Board of Railroad Commissioners Report,* 1890, 372.

2. Weller and Franzen, *Remembering the Southern Iowa Railway,* 1–16. On Gould, see Klein, *Jay Gould.*

3. Bennett and McLintock, "M&StL Railroad Co. History," 24; *Poor's Manual,* 1891, 255.

4. *Poor's Manual,* 1894, 225; *Poor's Manual,* 1891, 254–55; *Iowa Board of Railroad Commissioners Report,* 1890, 372; Donovan, *Mileposts,* 115; *Minneapolis Tribune,* August 21, 1895.

5. Illinois Railroad and Warehouse Commission, Annual Report, 1891, 85. This was the first dividend paid by the Iowa Central or any of its predecessors. *Poor's Manual,* 1897, 287; *Iowa Board of Railroad Commissioners Report,* 1890, 539.

6. *Iowa Board of Railroad Commissioners Report,* 1893, 82. According to *Iowa Board of Railroad Commissioners Reports,* in 1893 Iowa Central hauled a total of 572,586 passengers; 533,950 were local passengers, and only 38,686 were interline or through passengers. The cost of providing passenger service in 1893 was .0274 cents per passenger mile, as verified by the Iowa Board of Railroad Commissioners.

7. Iowa Central, Time Table, January 20, 1896,

5–8. *Minneapolis Tribune,* May 13, 1890; Bailey, *Compendium of Passenger Rates and Divisions,* 180–82; Iowa Central, Time Table, December 10, 1899, 4, 52.

8. Iowa Central, Time Table, May 14, 1897, passim.

9. Gerard Schultz, *History of Marshall County,* 41–42; Rosengren letter; Lynch interview; Overton interview; McCullen interview; Dold interview; Martin interview; Davison letter; Grimm, *Community History,* 73; *Gilman Dispatch,* undated clipping (1890s).

10. *Des Moines Leader,* April 24 and 27, 1898; *Waterloo Courier,* May 2, 1898.

11. *Marshalltown Times-Republican,* November 22, 1899.

12. Iowa Central, Annual Report, 1899, 8; Donovan, *Mileposts,* 119; Hocking Coal Co. Board Minutes.

13. Bateman et al., *Historical Encyclopedia,* vol. 1, 716.

14. Reed, *History of Kossuth County,* 456; Iowa Central, Annual Report, 1899, 11; *Poor's Manual,* 1912, 588–90.

15. Iowa Central, Time Table, December 10, 1899, 9–12, 51–54.

16. *Spencer News Herald,* March 29, 1899; Hofsommer, *Prairie Oasis,* 111; *Spirit Lake Beacon,* June 9 and August 4, 1899; *Estherville Vindicator,* July 15, 1899; *Journal of Commerce,* November 9, 1898.

17. *Official Guide,* January 1899, xxxii; 97 ICC 53–70; Lindsay and Maxwell, *History of the Muscatine,* 7–47.

18. Iowa Central, Annual Report, 1899, 5.

19. *Poor's Manual,* 588–90; *Iowa Board of Railroad Commissioners Report,* 1890, 539.

20. Bateman, *Historical Encyclopedia,* vol. 1, 716; *New York Times,* May 10, 1890.

9. Enter the Twentieth Century

1. Busbey, *Biographical Directory,* 263; Morell, *Diamond Jim,* 180; Hofsommer, "Edwin Hawley," 190–92.

2. Morell, *Diamond Jim,* 180; Coit, *Mr. Baruch,* 112–17.

3. Busbey, *Biographical Directory,* 263.

4. Iowa Central, Annual Report, 1900, 7.

5. Ibid., 1901, 12; *Minneapolis Tribune,* October 27, 1891; *Iowa Board of Railroad Commissioners Report,* 1895, xxxix–xi; *Iowa Board of Railroad Commissioners Report,* 1896, 175–76.

6. Iowa Central, Annual Report, 1901, 10, 13; Iowa Central, Annual Report, 1902, 5; *Railroad Gazette,* July 20, 1900, 488.

7. Iowa Central, Annual Report, 1903, 10.

8. Frances, *Universal Exposition of 1904,* vol. 1, 255–56, 259–60, 280, 452–58, 620–21, 627; H. Grant, Hofsommer, and Overby, *St. Louis Union Station,* 22–25.

9. *Poor's Manual,* 1911, 1233.

10. Iowa Central, Annual Report, 1906, 7, 9.

11. Moore, *Cab, Coach, and Caboose,* 135–39.

12. Sarnoff, *Russell Sage,* 326; Myers, *Great American Fortunes,* vol. 3, 57.

13. *Oskaloosa City Directory,* passim.

14. *Marshalltown Illustrated,* 8.

15. Ibid.

16. *Marshalltown Times-Republican,* March 27, 1900; Clarke letter.

17. Iowa Central, Annual Report, 1908, 7; *Marshalltown Times-Republican,* October 26, 1907; *Official Shippers' Guide and Directory,* passim; Young, *Taintor, Iowa,* 40–47; Iowa Central, Livestock Contracts.

18. *Official Railway Equipment Register,* June 1908, 241.

19. Traffic over the Keithsburg bridge normally was near the bottom as compared to traffic passing over the Mississippi River bridges of other Iowa carriers. However, as coal tonnage increased, the tonnage over the Keithsburg bridge surpassed that over the Illinois Central bridge at Dubuque and the Santa Fe structure at Fort Madison (1906 figures). Haynes, "History of Bridge"; Waddell, *Bridge Engineering,* vol. 1, 717–46.

20. Iowa Central, Annual Report, 1909, 11.

21. Swisher, "Mining in Iowa," 311–40; Schwieder, *Black Diamonds,* 3–58; Lees, "Coal Mining in Iowa," 545–50, 556–61; Olin, *Coal Mining in Iowa,* 44–59, 80–89; *History of Mahaska County* (1984), 2, 34–37, 197–203, 235–38; Cary, *Chicago, Milwaukee & St. Paul Railway,* 282–83; *Iowa Board of Railroad Commissioners Report,* 1903, 118.

22. *Iowa: Home for Immigrants,* 21; tabular data from Iowa Central annual reports, 1890–99, and from Iowa Railroad Commissioners reports, 1890–99; Swisher, "Mining in Iowa," 315–16.

23. Tabular data from Iowa Central annual reports,

1900–1911, and from Iowa Railroad Commissioners reports, 1900–1911.

24. Lynch interview, February 15, 1966; Mahaffey interview, February 15, 1966.

25. *Poor's Manual,* 1912, 1315.

26. Iowa Central, Annual Report, 1910, 8.

27. Data compiled from Iowa Railroad Commissioner Reports for the years indicated; J. H. McCarthy to All Agents, August 23, 1906.

28. Iowa Central, Revised Rules; Iowa Central, Wage Schedule; Iowa Central, Revised Rules; Iowa Central, Schedule for Engineers.

29. *Railway Age* 45 (August 14, 1908): 27–32; Iowa Central, Annual Report, 1910, 11; *New York Times,* October 9, 1908.

30. Donovan, *Mileposts,* 153.

31. Iowa Central, Annual Report, 1910, 8.

32. Donovan, *Mileposts,* 152.

33. *Centerville Iowegian,* Centennial Edition, November 29, 1946; *Poor's Manual,* 1912, 139; Boyle letter. See also Grant, "Electric Traction," 18–31.

34. Iowa Central, Annual Report, 1911, 10.

35. Donovan, *Mileposts,* 155, 161. On Newman Erb, see Boner, *Giant's Ladder,* 167, 170, 172.

36. M&StL, Time Table, 1904, 4–5.

37. Wabash Railroad, Time Table, January 1905, 2; Iowa Central, Time Table, October 1, 1905, passim; Iowa Central, Shipping Order, Winfield, Iowa, February 24, 1910; Iowa Central, Slip Bill for Empty Car Wabash 72277, February 10, 1910; *Marshalltown Times-Republican,* March 27, 1902.

38. *History of Mahaska County* (1984), 153–54; Peck interview; Wilson letters, May 23, 1949, and January 20, 1950; Pickett letter; Kingery, *Settlement to Centennial,* 42–45; 137 ICC 851–52; *Corwith, Iowa,* 16; C. S. Walters to All Agents; Greene letters.

39. Iowa Central, Time Table Number Fifty Seven (employee), December 17, 1911, passim.

40. Ibid.

41. Donovan, *Mileposts,* 155; *New York Times,* December 20, 1911; Butts, "Reminiscences," 6–15.

42. *Poor's Manual,* 1912, 1304; M&StL, Annual Report, 1912, 5.

Epilogue

1. Donovan, *Mileposts,* 99; Fuller, *John Muir of Wall Street,* 211–12.

2. Donovan, *Mileposts,* 180, 187.

3. M&StL, Annual Report, 1934, 39; 202 ICC 68–76; 207 ICC 459–68.

4. M&StL, Annual Report, 1939, p. 6, 1948, p. 9, 1952, p. 9; 99 ICC 526–28; 212 ICC 575–79; 228 ICC 459–60; 233 ICC 390–94.

5. *Minneapolis Tribune,* May 12–13, 1954; *New York Times,* May 12–13, 1954; *Des Moines Register,* April 24, 1954.

6. Donovan, *Mileposts,* 101; Grant, *The North Western,* 251–53.

BIBLIOGRAPHY

Books and Articles

Adler, Jeffrey S. *Yankee Merchants and the Making of the Urban West: Rise and Fall of Antebellum St. Louis.* New York: Cambridge University Press, 1991.

Agnew, Dwight L. "Beginnings of the Rock Island Lines." *Journal of Illinois State Historical Society* 46 (Winter 1953): 407–24.

Ambrose, Stephen E. *Nothing Like It in the World: Men Who Built the Transcontinental Railroad, 1863–1869.* New York: Simon & Schuster, 2000.

A. T. Andreas Illustrated Historical Atlas of the State of Iowa. Chicago: Andreas Atlas Co., 1875.

Bailey, W. F., comp. *The Compendium of Passenger Rates and Divisions.* Chicago: W. F. Bailey, 1897.

Bain, David Haward. *Empire Express: Building the First Transcontinental Railroad.* New York: Viking, 1999.

Baldwin, W. W., prep. *Corporate History of the Chicago, Burlington & Quincy Railroad Company and Affiliates.* Chicago: CB&Q, 1921.

Bassett, Isaac N. *Past and Present of Mercer County, Illinois.* 2 vols. Chicago: S. J. Clarke, 1914.

Bateman, Newton, et al., eds. *Historical Encyclopedia of Illinois and History of Warren County.* 2 vols. Chicago: Munsell Publishing, 1903.

Battin, William, and F. A. Moscrip. *Past and Present of Marshall County, Iowa.* 2 vols. Indianapolis: B. F. Bowen, 1912.

Beard, Earl S. "The Background of State Regulation in Iowa." *Iowa Journal of History* 51 (January 1953): 1–36.

———. "Local Aid to Railroads in Iowa." *Iowa Journal of History* 50 (January 1952): 1–34.

Belcher, Wyatt Winton. *The Economic Rivalry between St. Louis and Chicago, 1850–1880.* New York: Columbia University Press, 1947.

Biographical Directory of the Railway Officials of America. Title varies. Various editions, 1885–1912.

Biographical Historical Memoirs of Story County, Iowa. Chicago: Goodspeed Publishing, 1890.

Blegen, Theodore C. *Minnesota: A History of the State.* Minneapolis: University of Minnesota Press, 1963.

Boeck, George A. "A Decade of Transportation Fever in Burlington, 1845–1855." *Iowa Journal of History* 56 (April 1958): 129–52.

Boner, Harold F. *The Giant's Ladder.* Milwaukee: Kalmback Publishing, 1962.

Branch, E. Douglas. "The North Western." *Palimpsest* 10 (June 1929): 212–18.

Bryant, Ray L. *A Preliminary Guide to Iowa Railroads, 1850–1972.* Iowa City: Privately produced, 1984.

Busbey, T. Addison, comp. and ed. *The Biographical Directory of the Railway Officials of America.* Chicago: Railway Age, 1906.

Butts, A. P. "Reminiscences." *Switch Lamp,* January 1967, 6–15.

Campbell, E. G. *The Reorganization of the American Railroad System, 1893–1900.* New York: Columbia University Press, 1938.

Carlson, Norman, ed. *Iowa Trolleys.* Chicago: Central Electric Railfans' Association, 1975.

Carr, Hobart C. *Early History of Iowa Railroads.* New York: Arno Press, 1981.

Cary, John W. *The Organization and History of the Chicago, Milwaukee & St. Paul Railway Company.* Chicago: Cramer, Aikens & Cramer, 1893.

Casey, Robert J., and W. A. Douglas. *Pioneer Railroad: The Story of the Chicago & North Western System.* New York: McGraw-Hill, 1948.

Chandler, Alfred E. Jr. *The Visible Hand: The Managerial Revolution in American Business.* Cambridge, MA: Harvard University Press, 1977.

Chapman, John Will. *Railroad Mergers.* New York: Simmons-Boardman, 1934.

Cochran, Thomas C. *Business Leaders, 1845–1890: The Business Mind in Action.* Cambridge, MA: Harvard University Press, 1953.

Coit, Margaret L. *Mr. Baruch.* Boston: Houghton Mifflin, 1957.

Cole, Cyrenus. *Iowa through the Years.* Iowa City: State Historical Society of Iowa, 1940.

Cooper, Claire C. "The Role of Railroads in the Settlement of Iowa: A Study in Historical Geography." Unpublished master's thesis, University of Nebraska, Lincoln, 1958.

Corliss, Carlton J. *Main Line of Mid-America: The Story of the Illinois Central Railroad.* New York: Creative Age Press, 1950.

Corwith, Iowa—"Then" and "Now." Corwith: Corwith Centennial Committee, 1980.

Cronon, William. *Nature's Metropolis: Chicago and the Great West.* New York: W. W. Norton, 1991.

Cuniff, M. G. "Increasing Railroad Consolidation." *World's Work* 3 (Fall 1902): 1775–80.

Davis, Cullom. "Illinois: Crossroads and Cross Section." In *Heartland: Comparative Histories of the Midwestern States.* Bloomington: Indiana University Press, 1988, 127–57.

Derleth, August. *The Milwaukee Road: Its First 100 Years.* New York: Creative Age Press, 1948.

Donovan, Frank P., Jr. "The Amazing Great Western." *Railroad Magazine* 61 (September 1953): 13–18.

———. *Mileposts on the Prairie: The Story of the Minneapolis & St. Louis Railway.* New York: Simmons-Boardman, 1950.

———. "The Wabash in Iowa." *Palimpsest* 45 (October 1964): 369–400.

Douglas, George H. *The Railroad in American Life.* New York: Paragon Press, 1992.

Fels, Rendig. *American Business Cycles, 1865–1897.* Chapel Hill: University of North Carolina Press, 1959.

Foster, Mrs. J. E., ed. *Franklin County History, 1852–1970.* Hampton: Franklin County Historical Society, 1970.

Francaviglia, Richard V., and Jimmy L. Bryan Jr. "'Are We Chimerical in This Opinion?' Visions of a Pacific Railroad and Westward Expansion before 1845." *Pacific Historical Review* 71 (May 2002): 179–202.

Frances, David R. *The Universal Exposition of 1904.* 2 vols. St. Louis: Louisiana Exposition Company, 1913.

Freidel, Frank. *The Splendid Little War.* Boston: Little, Brown, 1958.

Fuller, Muriel O. *John Muir of Wall Street.* New York: Knickerbocker Press, 1927.

Gates, Paul Wallace. "The Railroads of Missouri, 1860–1870." *Missouri Historical Review* 26 (January 1932): 126–41.

Glaab, Charles N. *Kansas City and the Railroads: Community Policy in the Growth of a Regional Metropolis.* Lawrence: University Press of Kansas, 1993.

Grant, H. Roger. "A. B. Stickney Builds a Railroad: The Saga of the Minnesota & Northwestern." *Midwest Review* 6 (Spring 1984): 13–26.

———, ed. *Brownie the Boomer: The Life of Charles P. Brown, an American Railroader.* DeKalb: Northern Illinois University Press, 1991.

———. *The Corn Belt Route: A History of the Chicago Great Western Railroad Company.* DeKalb: Northern Illinois University Press, 1984.

———. "Electric Traction Promotion in the South Iowa Coal Fields." *Palimpsest* 58 (January–February 1971): 18–32.

———. *The North Western: A History of the Chicago & North Western Railway System.* DeKalb: Northern Illinois University Press, 1996.

Grant, H. Roger, Don L. Hofsommer, and Osmund Overby. *St. Louis Union Station: A Place for People, a Place for Trains*. St. Louis: St. Louis Mercantile Library, 1994.

Grimm, Donald H. *Community History: Zearing, Iowa.* Zearing: Privately published by the author, 1956.

Grinnell, Josiah Bushnell. *Men and Events of Forty Years.* Boston: D. Lothrop, 1891.

Grodinsky, Julius. *Jay Gould: His Business Career, 1867–1892.* Philadelphia: University of Pennsylvania Press, 1957.

Harlow, Alvin F. *Steelways of New England.* New York: Creative Age Press, 1946.

Havinghurst, Walter. *Land of Promise: The Story of the Northwest Territory.* New York: N.p., 1946.

Hayes, William Edward. *Iron Road to Empire: The History of the Rock Island Lines.* New York: Simmons-Boardman, 1953.

Haynes, R. C. "History of Bridge over the Mississippi River at Keithsburg, Illinois." Minneapolis and St. Louis Railway, Minneapolis, July 22, 1949, mimeo.

Heacock, C. C. *Local Reminiscences of the Early History of Brighton, Iowa.* Brighton, IA: Enterprise Press, 1900.

Hickenlooper, Frank. *An Illustrated History of Monroe County, Iowa.* Kansas City: Hudson-Kimberly, 1896.

Hill, Howard C. "The Development of Chicago as a Center of Meat Packing Industry." *Mississippi Valley Historical Review* 10 (December 1923): 253–73.

Hilton, George W. *American Narrow Gauge Railroads.* Stanford, CA: Stanford University Press, 1990.

Hilton, George W., and John F. Due. *The Electric Interurban Railway in America.* Stanford, CA: Stanford University Press, 1960.

History of Hardin County. Springfield, IL: Union Publishing, 1883.

History of Kossuth and Humboldt Counties, Iowa. Springfield, IL: Union Publishing, 1884.

History of Mahaska County, Iowa. Des Moines, IA: Union Historical Co., 1878.

History of Mahaska County, Iowa. Dallas, TX: Curtis Media Corp., 1984.

History of Marshall County, Iowa. Chicago: Western Historical Co., 1878.

History of Mercer County. Chicago: H. H. Hill & Co., 1882.

History of Mitchell and Worth Counties, Iowa. Springfield, IL: Union Publishing, 1884.

History of Monroe County, Iowa. Chicago: Western Historical Company, 1878.

History of Poweshiek County, Iowa. Des Moines, IA: Union Historical, Birdsall, Williams, 1880.

History of Roland, Iowa, 1870–1970. Roland, IA: Privately published, 1970.

History of the Wabash Railroad. St. Louis: Wabash, 1953.

Hoffman, Phil. *Oskaloosa—Or, the First One Hundred Years in a Midwestern Town.* Cedar Rapids, IA: Torch Press, 1942.

Hofsommer, Don L. "Edwin Hawley." In *Railroads in the Age of Regulation, 1900–1980,* ed. Keith L. Bryant. New York: Facts on File, 1988, 190–92.

———. "The Grandest Railroad Project of the Age." *Annals of Iowa* 44 (Fall 1977): 118–36.

———. "A History of the Iowa Central Railway." Unpublished master's thesis, State College of Iowa, Cedar Falls, 1966.

———. *Prairie Oasis: The Railroads, Steamboats, and Resorts of Iowa's Spirit Lake Country.* Des Moines: Waukon & Mississippi Press, 1975.

———. "The Railroad and an Iowa Editor: A Case Study." *Annals of Iowa* 41 (Fall 1972): 1073–1103.

Iowa: The Home for Immigrants. Des Moines: Iowa Board of Immigration, 1870.

Johnson, Jack T. "Plumbe's Railroad to the Moon." *Palimpsest* 19 (March 1938): 89–97.

Kennan, George. *E. E. Harriman: A Biography.* 2 vols. Boston: Houghton Mifflin, 1922.

King, John. "John Plumbe: Originator of the Pacific Railroad." *Annals of Iowa* 6 (January 1904): 288–96.

Kingery, Karlene, ed. *Settlement to Centennial: History of St. Anthony Area from Time of Earliest Settlement, 1849–1982.* St. Anthony, IA: St. Anthony Centennial Committee, 1982.

Klein, Maury. *Life and Legend of E. E. Harriman.* Chapel Hill: University of North Carolina Press, 2000.

———. *The Life and Legend of Jay Gould.* Baltimore: Johns Hopkins University Press, 1986.

Larson, Arthur Q. "Platt Smith of Dubuque: His Early Career." *Palimpsest* 58 (May–June 1977): 88–96.

Lees, James H. "History of Coal Mining in Iowa." *Iowa Geological Survey* 22 (1913): 525–88.

Lewis, S. Thompson, ed. *History of Appanoose and Monroe Counties, Iowa.* New York: Lewis Publishing, 1903.

Lindsay, Bill, and Brent Maxwell. *The History of the Muscatine North and South Railroad Co.* Burlington, IA: Privately published by the authors, 1997.

Long, Bryant Alden, and William Jefferson Dennis. *Mail by Rail: The Story of the Postal Transportation Service.* New York: Simmons-Boardman, 1951.

Lota, David, and Charles Franzen. *Rails to a County Seat.* Washington, IA: Privately published by the authors, 1989.

Lotz, David E. "The Burlington & Western and Burlington & Northwestern Narrow Gauge Lines." *Burlington Bulletin* (December 1994): 4–27.

Marshalltown Illustrated. Marshalltown, IA: Times-Republican Printing, 1907.

Martin, Albro. *Railroads Triumphant: The Growth, Rejection, and Rebirth of a Vital American Force.* New York: Oxford University Press, 1991.

McKee, Leo A., and Alfred L. Lewis, eds. *Railroad Post Office History.* Pleasantville, NY: Mobile Post Office Society, 1972.

Means, O. H. "The Minneapolis & St. Louis Railroad Company." *Bulletin 31* (Railway & Locomotive Historical Society) (April 1933): 33–45.

Meyer, Balthasar Henry. *Railway Legislation in the United States.* New York: Macmillan, 1903.

Moore, Al. *Cab, Coach, and Caboose.* Des Moines, IA: Welch Printing, 1902.

Morell, Parker. *Diamond Jim.* Garden City, NY: Garden City Publishing, 1934.

Myers, Gustavus. *History of the Great American Fortunes.* 3 vols. Chicago: Charles H. Kerr, 1917.

Neill, Edward W. *History of Freeborn County.* Minneapolis: Minnesota Historical Co., 1882.

Newcomb, H. T. "The Recent Great Railroad Combinations." *Review of Reviews* 24 (August 1901): 163–74.

Norem, Enoch A., comp. "The Mason City Story," *Mason City Globe-Gazette,* Centennial Edition, July 1, 1953.

Oberholtzer, Ellis P. *Jay Cooke: Financier of the Civil War.* 2 vols. Philadelphia: George W. Jacobs, 1907.

Olin, Hubert L. *Coal Mining in Iowa.* Des Moines: Iowa Department of Mines and Minerals, 1965.

One Hundredth Anniversary, 1981: The Winfield Beacon. Winfield, IA: Winfield Beacon, 1981.

Oskaloosa City Directory 1900–1901. Oskaloosa, IA: Shockley Bros. & Cook, 1901.

Overton, Richard C. *Burlington Route: A History of the Burlington Lines.* New York: Alfred A. Knopf, 1965.

Parker, Leonard F. *History of Poweshiek County, Iowa.* Chicago: S. J. Clarke Publishing, 1911.

The Past and Present of Warren County, Illinois. Chicago: H. F. Kett, 1877.

Payne, Charles R. *Josiah Bushnell Grinnell.* Iowa City: State Historical Society of Iowa, 1938.

Poor's Manual of the Railroads of the United States. Title varies; issued annually, 1870–1912.

Portrait and Biographical Album of Warren County, Illinois. Chicago: Chapman Brothers, 1886.

Preston, Ruth I. "The Lyons and Iowa Central Railroad." *Annals of Iowa* 9 (January 1910): 284–301.

Pride in Our Past: A Pictorial History of Franklin County, Iowa. Hampton, IA: Hampton Chronicle & Times, 1996.

Primm, James Neal. *Lion of the Valley: St. Louis, Missouri.* Boulder, CO: Pruett Publishing, 1990.

Reavis, L. U. *The Railway and River Systems of the City of St. Louis.* St. Louis: Woodward, Tiernan & Hale, 1879.

Reed, Benjamin. *History of Kossuth County, Iowa.* Chicago: S. J. Clarke Publishing, 1913.

Rose and Thorns of Yesteryear. Searsboro, IA: Searsboro Centennial Committee, 1970.

Sage, Leland L. *History of Iowa.* Ames: Iowa State University Press, 1974.

———. *William Boyd Allison: A Study in Practical Politics.* Iowa City: State Historical Society of Iowa, 1956.

Sarnoff, Paul. *Russell Sage: The Money King.* New York: Ivan Obolensky, 1965.

Saunders, Richard. *Merging Lines: American Railroads, 1900–1970.* DeKalb: Northern Illinois University Press, 2001.

Schultz, Gerard. *History of Marshall County, Iowa.* Marshalltown, IA: Marshall Printing, 1955.

Schwieder, Dorothy. *Black Diamonds: Life and Work in Iowa's Coal Mining Communities, 1895–1925.* Ames: Iowa State University Press, 1983.

Smalley, E. V., comp. *Northern Pacific Railroad Book of Reference.* New York: E. Wells Sackett & Rankin, 1883.

Stover, John F. *American Railroads.* 2nd ed. Chicago: University of Chicago Press, 1997.

———. *History of the Illinois Central Railroad.* New York: Macmillan, 1975.

———. *Iron Road to the West: American Railroads in the l850s.* New York: Columbia University Press, 1978.

Stuart, I. L., ed. *History of Franklin County, Iowa.* 2 vols. Chicago: S. J. Clarke Publishing, 1914.

Swartz, William. "The Wabash Railroad." *Railroad History* (Fall 1975): 1–35.

Swisher, Jacob A. "Mining in Iowa." *Iowa Journal of History* 43 (October 1945): 305–56.

Taylor, George Rogers. *The Transportation Revolution, 1815–1860.* New York: Holt, Rinehart & Winston, 1915.

Taylor, George Rogers, and Irene D. Neu. *The American Railroad Network, 1861–1890.* Cambridge, MA: Harvard University Press, 1956.

Taylor, L. L., ed. *Past and Present of Appanoose County, Iowa.* Chicago: S. J. Clarke Publishing, 1913.

Thompson, William H. *Transportation in Iowa: A Historical Summary.* Ames: Iowa Department of Transportation, 1989.

Toussaint, Willard I. "Charles Mason and the Burlington Northwestern Narrow Gauge Railroad." *Annals of Iowa* 38 (Winter 1966): 185–203.

Waddell, J. A. L. *Bridge Engineering.* 2 vols. New York: John Wiley & Sons, 1916.

Wall, Joseph Frazier. *Iowa: A History.* New York: W. W. Norton, 1978.

Ward, James A. "On Time: Railroads and the Tempo of American Life." *Railroad History* (Autumn 1984): 87–95.

———. *Railroads and the Character of America, 1820–1887.* Knoxville: University of Tennessee Press, 1986.

Weller, Peter, and Charles Franzen. *Remembering the Southern Iowa Railway: A Pictorial History.* Washington, IA: Privately published by the authors, 1992.

Welles, H. T. *Autobiography and Reminiscences.* 2 vol. Minneapolis: Marshall Robinson, 1899.

Wilson, Ben Hur. "The Narrow Gauge." *Palimpsest* 13 (April 1932): 151–53.

Wright, Luella M. *Peter Melendy.* Iowa City: State Historical Society of Iowa, 1943.

Yesterday and Today: A History of the Chicago & North Western System. Chicago: C&NW, 1910.

Young, Beverly Sue. *Taintor, Iowa:* N.p., N.d.

Newspapers and Periodicals

Ackley (Iowa) World Journal, 1957

Albia (Iowa) Union, 1866

Belmond (Iowa) Herald, 1881

Belmond (Iowa) Independent, 1925

Boston Transcript, 1871–87

Cedar Falls (Iowa) Gazette, 1864–11

Centerville Iowegian, 1946

Chicago Tribune, 1886–90

Des Moines Leader, 1898

Eldora (Iowa) Ledger, 1866–68

Estherville Vindicator, 1899

Gilman (Iowa) Dispatch, 1890s

Grinnell (Iowa) Herald-Register, 1958

Journal of Commerce, 1898

Marshalltown (Iowa) Times-Republican, 1899, 1900, 1953

Mason City (Iowa) Globe-Gazette, 1953

Minneapolis Tribune, 1879–1895

New York Times, 1882, 1908, 1911

Official Guide of the Railways, monthly, 1870–1912; title varies

Official Railway Equipment Register, monthly, 1908

Oskaloosa (Iowa) Herald, 1866

Poweshiek County (Iowa) Journal, 1871

Railroad Gazette, 1881–1900

Railway Age, 1908

Railway World, 1880

Spencer (Iowa) News Herald, 1899

Spirit Lake (Iowa) Beacon, 1899

Toledo (Iowa) Chronicle, 1950

Waterloo (Iowa) Courier, 1898

Government Reports

Illinois Railroad and Warehouse Commission, Annual Reports, 1874–91

Interstate Commerce Commission, *Valuation Reports* 137: 870–71

Iowa Board of Railroad Commissioners Reports, 1878–1912; title varies

Manuscript Collections

Albert N. Harbert Collection, Special Collections, University of Iowa Libraries, Iowa City

James J. Hill Collection, Hill Reference Library, St. Paul

Levi O. Leonard Collection, Special Collections, University of Iowa Libraries, Iowa City

Northern Pacific Collection, Minnesota Historical Society, St. Paul

Company Materials or Publications

Bennett, F. K., and J. S. McLintock. "The M&StL Railroad Co. History." Minneapolis: Minneapolis & St. Louis, 1921.

Central Iowa Railway. Annual Report, 1882.

———. *The Great Northwest* (pamphlet), 1887.

———. Time Tables, 1884, 1886.

Central Railroad Company of Iowa. Articles of Incorporation, 1869.

———. Compromise Measure, June 1875.

———. Locomotive Statement for the Month of August 1871.

———. Memorandum Guide, 1874.

———. Receivers Report, August 31, 1877.

———. Report of the Boston Committee to Bondholders, 1875.

———. Report of Earnings for the Month of October, 1871.

———. Value and Security of Its First Mortgage Seven Per Cent. Gold Bonds, September 15, 1869; March 1, 1870; June 20, 1870; October 1, 1870.

———. Weekly Local Ticket Report, Searsboro, Iowa, March 31, 1872.

Chicago & North Western. *Abandonments Book.* Reproduced by the Chicago & North Western Historical Society, 1999.

Chicago, Milwaukee & St. Paul, Central Railroad Company of Iowa, and St. Louis, Kansas City & Northern. Time Schedule through between St. Paul and Minneapolis, St. Louis and Kansas City, June 1878.

Chicago, Rock Island & Pacific. Annual Report, 1870. Author's collection.

Hocking Coal Company. Board Minutes, 1898. Chicago & Northwestern Secretary's Office, Chicago.

Iowa Central. Annual Reports, 1870–1911 (includes reports of predecessor railroads).

———. Livestock Contracts, Olds and Wayland, Iowa, 1899–1908.

———. J. H. McCarthy to All Agents, August 23, 1906. Author's collection.

———. Revised Rules Relating to Enginemen, February 1, 1893.

———. Schedule for Engineers, Firemen, Conductors, and Brakemen, January 1, 1907.

———. Shipping Order, Winfield, Iowa, February 24, 1910.

———. Slip Bill for Empty Car Wabash 72277, February 10, 1910.

———. Time Tables, 1874–1911 (includes time tables of predecessor railroads).

———. Wage Schedule for Locomotive Enginemen, June 15, 1903.

———. C. S. Walters to All Agents, August 1, 1908. Author's collection.

Iowa River Railway. Prospectus, 1869.

Minneapolis & St. Louis. Annual Reports, 1899–1912.

———. Search of Records Document, October 1920.

———. Time Tables, 1904.

Northern Pacific Railroad. Report of the Chief Engineer on the Unfinished Portion of the Railroad, April 27, 1874.

Official Shippers' Guide and Directory of the Minneapolis & St. Louis Railroad and Iowa Central Railway. Chicago: Perk-Hill, 1909.

St. Louis, Iowa and Minnesota R.R. Co. Prospectus: Designed to Be a Successor to the Central Railroad Company of Iowa, 1875.

Wabash Railroad. Time Tables, 1905.

Interviews and Correspondence

J. P. Boyle, general manager of the Iowa Southern Utilities Company, letter to D. G. Fisher, president of the Iowa Southern Utilities Company, March 15, 1921.

Edward Bray, former Minneapolis & St. Louis station agent, interview, Winfield, Iowa, September 1, 1965.

T. E. Clarke, letter to C. J. Ives, March 28, 1900. Albert N. Harbert Collection (MsC434).

W. Russell Davison, letter to the author, June 19, 1972.

George F. Dold, interview, Coppock, Iowa, May 17, 1972.

Lida Lisle Greene, letters to the author, December 19, 1990; January 5, 1992.

Martin Grinde, former Minneapolis & St. Louis section foreman, interview, Ackley, Iowa, February 21, 1965.

P. C. Heninger, retired farmer, interview, Martinsburg, Iowa, August 30, 1965.

Frank Lynch, former Iowa Central brakeman, interview, Marshalltown, Iowa, February 15, 1965.

Merle Mahaffey, former Iowa Central fireman, interview, Marshalltown, Iowa, February 15, 1965.

Mrs. Fern Martin, interview, Hampton, Iowa, September 1, 1965.

Mrs. Minnie McCullen, interview, Coppock, Iowa, May 14, 1972.

Al Overton, former Minneapolis & St. Louis agent, interview, London Mills, Illinois, August 31, 1965.

Joe Peck, former Minneapolis & St. Louis agent, interview, Dillon, Iowa, February 9, 1966.

Clarence E. Pickett, letter to Frank P. Donovan Jr., December 18, 1950.

Mrs. M. W. Rosengren, letter to the author, June 15, 1965.

Paul H. Stringham, letter to the author, March 14, 1966.

Sturm, James L. "Railroads and Market Growth: The Case of Peoria and Chicago, 1850–1900." Unpublished master's thesis, University of Wisconsin, Madison, 1965.

Ben H. Wilson, letters to Frank P. Donovan Jr., May 23, 1949; January 20, 1950; December 18, 1950.

Index

Don L. Hofsommer is professor of history at St. Cloud State University. He is a native Iowan who was born at Fort Dodge, grew up at Spencer, and graduated from the University of Northern Iowa at Cedar Falls. He is the author and coauthor of several books, including *The Tootin' Louie: A History of the Minneapolis & St. Louis Railway, The Great Northern Railway: A History,* and *Minneapolis and the Age of Railways,* all published by the University of Minnesota Press.

OTHER UNIVERSITY OF MINNESOTA PRESS BOOKS OF INTEREST